bush
PUBLISHING
& associates

Presented To:

From:

Date:

Books and Business Curriculum

by Margo Bush

Dream Big, Live Big!

Win Your Mile

Don't Do Business Alone Elite Business Apprentice Program

The Road to Growth Program

Church Administration Resource Manual

DREAM BIG, LIVE BIG!

How Having The Proper Tools And Proper Business Principles Changed My Life, Business, Increased Sales, And Provided Financial Security.

YOU CAN DO IT TOO

MARGO BUSH

bush
PUBLISHING
& associates

DREAM BIG, LIVE BIG!

ISBN (paperback) 978-1-63821-357-4
ISBN (ebook) 978-1-63821-358-1

Copyright © 2021 by Dr. Margo Bush

All rights reserved. No part of this book may be reproduced, stored in a retrieval system or transmitted in any form or by any means, electronic, photocopied, recorded or otherwise, without the prior permission in writing of the publisher, except for the use of brief quotations in a book review. For more information, contact Bush Publishing and Associates, LLC.

First printing 2021 by
Bush Publishing and Associates, LLC
Tulsa, Oklahoma
www.bushpublishing.com
info@bushpublishing.com

Margo Bush can be reached at 405-492-2805 or at margo@bushpublishing.com

Bush Publishing & Associates, LLC., books may be ordered at bookstores everywhere and through Amazon.com.

Cover Art, Layout and Design by Bush Publishing and Associates, LLC, Tulsa, Oklahoma

Editing by Writing By Michele, LLC, Tulsa, Oklahoma

Printed in the United States of America.

DEDICATION

Thank you to all of the business owners, authors, and leaders I have coached, consulted and counseled over more than three decades of my career. You have taught me more than I have ever taught you about friendship, life, and living. You've helped me make the most of my journey and to live out my divine purpose in helping people win. This book would not have been written if you had not given me the opportunity to coach and mentor you.

    I dedicate this book to one of the most amazing mentors I have had in my life. You held my hand and taught me the basics of business in the most difficult time of my life. You were a God send when life began to look very different. My businesses would not be what they are today without you and your teaching gift. Dan Vega, I owe the foundation of my success in business to you. Thank you.

PREFACE

If you have picked up this book, then I believe you have selected it because you are looking for answers. You're ready to find greater success in life and in business. You may be wondering whether you even have what it takes to build a successful business. I am here to tell you: YES, YOU DO! You will need some help along the way, but that is why I've written this book. I want to help you achieve your goals.

I've been right where you are, asking these same questions. I was desperate and didn't know who to turn to for real business answers. My small publishing company was just barely making it—but I wanted it to thrive. In fact, a day came when I desperately needed it to grow if I was going to support myself and my children after my husband unexpectedly died. At the time, I was in my forties, lost, heartbroken and hurting. I felt like my life had been thrown off track. I had so many questions—questions you have probably asked yourself as well.

If others are able to build successful businesses that serve their families well, then why can't the rest of us achieve that too? We all have the same twenty-four hours in a day to succeed in life. So, why are some people doing better in their business than others?

Why are some business owners barely making payroll while others are thriving? What principles are in practice—or not in practice—that are making the difference between dying or thriving, barely surviving, or living to the fullest? Is there a different set of rules the best CEOs are playing by? Or, are there just simple rules that small business owners don't know or have never been taught? You started your business with passion, and you thought if you built it, people would come. When they didn't come and you weren't making any money, why not? You work hard every day, but nothing is changing in your bank account.

I believed there was more. In my desperation to build a life and business that would support me and my family, I began to look for answers. Those answers are the basis of this book and the answer to the questions I hear every day from struggling business owners across this country—principles that I believe will turn your business around, so it, and you, can truly thrive.

These principles changed my life and my business. That's why I wrote this book—so you can have the tools and knowledge you need to begin to build and enjoy success, the financial future you desire, one that reflects your hard work as an entrepreneur.

As we take this journey together, I encourage you to stay open to new ideas. Expect to discover things that may challenge you and change the ways you have always been taught about business that maybe, just maybe weren't right. I believe if you will take a chance on a new way of thinking about how to do business, it will ultimately bring about big results. Expect to learn how to truly take your business to the next level and dream big.

That's my sincere desire for you—and I'm excited to take this exciting journey with you to more success in business.

For Your Success,

Margo Bush

TABLE OF CONTENTS

DEDICATION..ix

PREFACE..xi

CHAPTER ONE: Dream Big..1
If you're going to live big, you first must dream bigger than you've ever dreamed before.

CHAPTER TWO: Interrupted 9
Because life and business will go wrong, you have to be ready to dig deep to pursue your dreams.

CHAPTER THREE: Opportunity Awaits..21
It's when we rise to the occasion that great things can happen in our lives and in our businesses.

CHAPTER FOUR: The Art of People...35
Dreaming big and living big requires us to learn how to truly understand ourselves and others.

CHAPTER FIVE: It's All in the Math...49
Before you can achieve big things in business, you must change how you think about the numbers of doing business.

CHAPTER SIX: Master Your Business 59

To reach your big goals, sometimes you have to unlearn wrong concepts, dig deep to find the right information, be courageous and forge your own path.

CHAPTER SEVEN: Write the Vision 71

Failure to plan wisely and thoroughly can derail any business, so you must create a clear vision that you can follow.

CHAPTER EIGHT: Your Next Level 79

Accomplishing more through your business and hitting bigger goals means you must take new actions to produce the results you're looking for.

CHAPTER NINE: Direct Sales 87

To ensure you are on your way to success as you define it, you must embrace the power of selling—and develop confidence in your ability to market yourself.

CHAPTER TEN: Enjoy the Journey 95

The journey you're on is bigger than your business. Don't miss out on the full picture of life that is available to you.

SUCCESS

To laugh often, love more, work hard
enjoy the journey and have fun doing it.
To win the respect of men, women, friends
family and intelligent people.
To earn the appreciation of the honest critics
and endure the betrayal of friends and family.
To appreciate beauty, the world and the
wonders He has made to enjoy.
To contribute to humanity and leave the world
and those around you a little bit better.
To learn from your mistakes and have
the strength to overcome them.

To become better and give more.
To not quit or give up when those who
matter most can't celebrate you.
To learn to listen to those who do.
To know even one life has breathed easier
because you have lived, loved and given.
This is to have succeeded.

Based on the writings of
Elisabeth-Anne Anderson Stanley, and Ralph Waldo Emerson

CHAPTER ONE

Dream Big

The most courageous act is still to think for yourself. **Aloud.**
—COCO CHANEL, fashion designer and businesswoman

Is there a financial roulette table somewhere that determines who will become successful and who will not? Who can grow a profitable business, and who can't? Does wealth come from being smarter and working harder, or are certain people just destined to have more than others? Is success based on gender or dependent on marital status? Does prosperity happen because one might look prettier, live on the right side of the street, or be more gifted than someone else? Or could there be other factors that play a role in your success?

If you're like me, you've probably asked similar questions as you considered where you are in your life and your business. Most of us want success and we may even dream big—but so many times, we don't know how to turn those dreams into reality.

The bottom line—and what this book is all about—is this: *You* are the CEO of your own life. You—yes, you—have been entrusted with the life you've been given. What will you do with it? What will you set out to accomplish with the gifts you have been given?

Making a decision to take control of our lives and our businesses isn't always easy, especially when things don't go as we have planned. And believe me, CEO of our own life or not, we will all experience times when things go awry. In those times, it will be more important than ever to push forward toward success. Don't let past circumstances in your life keep you from having all you can have or fulfilling your divine destiny.

How do I know this? Because it happened to me. And it happens to others. Life can interrupt our dreams, and that leaves us with a choice to make about how we'll move forward. The way we come to the point of decision may differ, but the result is the same: we find ourselves facing a situation that demands we dig deep to survive and thrive. To not stay stuck in past losses or past hurts, but to move on with our lives and all that we are called to do. For me an unexpected death, lifelong plans interrupted, and grief called my name every day for years to hold on to what I had lost. Every day I fought to not listen to it, look forward and not keep looking back.

For me, this happened in the fall of 2009, when everything in my life changed in a matter of one unexpected moment. Before that day, it seemed as if my future had been carved out; life was fairly easy and smooth. Little did I know what was ahead, and how vital it would become for me to dream again and see life bigger in order to secure a future I could be proud of.

In other words, everything you're about to read in this book is the result of lessons I've learned, many of them the hard way. I know these principles for life and business work, because I've lived them. And you can learn them too. You, too, can dream big and fulfill your God-given destiny. Your business, and your life, can thrive and be as big as you want them to be. But you have to choose it and pursue it, because it will not happen by accident. It requires effort and disciplined mastery of your business to make it happen.

MAKE YOUR CHOICE

A businessman once said to me, "If you will listen to me and do everything I tell you to do, you will be set for life."

At that time, the very idea of being set for life seemed impossible—yet I knew I needed a drastic change in my circumstances. The business that had been laid in my lap to run was suffering. I had just lost my husband, and the grief was more than anyone should be expected to handle. I could hardly get out of bed each morning, even though my business needed my full attention. Most days, I cried so hard that my heart felt like it was going to come out of my chest. Whenever I worked late at the office, driving home in the evening became a challenge because the lines in the road disappeared for all the tears I was shedding.

Beyond my obvious and understandable grief, I also faced fear, confusion, and a sense of overwhelm at the thought of the future. I had been a pastor's wife for years and had helped run a growing ministry. But it all seemed like second nature, and I didn't really know how it translated into corporate America. All I knew was that I had worked hard at serving people. Even if I gave up my business and looked for a job, I wondered who would hire someone who had no real corporate experience.

I was facing the reality of taking care of myself and a teenage son, something I had never had to do alone before, and it frightened me. How was I going to survive? Desperate, I knew I had to find the courage to walk a new road in life and business that I had never before walked.

You may find yourself in a similar bind. Many of us are. Statistically, fifty percent of businesses that open today will close within one to three years. There is something desperately wrong with those numbers when we have the ability to access massive amounts of information, most of it for free. The information is out there. Yet three percent of the people in this country have more wealth than the remaining ninety-seven percent combined. Why is this?

Here's what I know: No one opens a business just to close it down. Yet more than 400,000 businesses close each year. Why is that? And what can you do to avoid being one of those statistics?

It's time to learn how to grow your business properly, so you can genuinely succeed at being an entrepreneur rather than barely making it. Listen, if you want to work from home and make a good living, you can. If you want to make money doing what you love and running your own business, you can. If you want to grow an empire and put lots of people to work, you can. It is not only possible but probable—when you know and execute the proper principles for business success. You can learn how to build a strong company, grow for future returns, and do it the right way, without compromising your ethics.

When I found myself facing my own choice of whether I would learn everything possible to make my business thrive, I had no idea of the great adventure I was about to embark upon. I had no idea how much I didn't know about proper business practices. Not long after I started seeking solutions that would grow my business, a set of what I call miraculous events began to happen that gave me the opportunity to learn the proper tools and business principles that would change my life.

Over the course of the next few years, a framework for business emerged for me, one that would really work. I felt like a new baby beginning to walk. But I leaned into it. In the course of this learning process, I had some wins and some failures. I didn't do everything right, but who does? We all have to get over our failures and move on to the next task. If you've had failures, it's time to let them go and use this time, this book, to help you move forward.

SUCCESS IS UP TO US

Don't be intimidated by what you don't know. That can be your greatest strength and ensure that you do things differently from everyone else.
—SARA BLAKELY, founder of Spanx

It is my hope that in the pages ahead, you will see the thread woven throughout your own journey that has prepared you to go bigger, do more, and have the courage to build your own dreams. My goal is that this book will fill in the holes that may be missing in your business education right now and equip you to know how to take your business or organization to the next level.

In other words, may this book and the knowledge in it serve as a destined opportunity for you to move ahead in life and business. May it help you to have the courage to go beyond the broken heart, the fear of never having enough, so you can live bigger than the obstacles you may be facing. These are not just your dreams we're talking about—they are your destiny.

Just remember, if your name is on it, then it's no one else's but yours. And you deserve to pursue it with everything within you until you accomplish all you are destined to do.

Oh, and by the way, I listened to my friend and followed his business advice. Within three months I had tripled my profits, and by the end of that first year I had paid off all the debts in my business. It was a joyful milestone in my life, something I had never done on my own before, so needless to say, I was ecstatic. That year, I closed the door on scarcity and never looked back.

Over the next few years, I learned how to run a business, what to do and what not to do. Watching and learning what worked and what didn't work was the best on-the-job training anyone could ever have in order to grow a business. What I learned, I'm now sharing with you, so that you do not have to do it alone, as I did.

My hope is this, that these principles will give you the tools and education you need to grow beyond where you are today and give you hope when you are frustrated and struggling, like they did me. If you are looking for answers and you stay open, opportunities to move closer to your destiny will be there for you at just the right time. I believe this book is one of those opportunities. May these principles and insights serve you as well as they have served me—so you can dream and live as big as you want to.

CHAPTER TWO

Interrupted

What I wanted was to be allowed to do the thing in the world that I did best—which I believed then and believe now is the greatest privilege there is. When I did that, success found me.
—DEBBI FIELDS, creator of Mrs. Fields

You can be going through daily life, doing business as usual, when it all suddenly and unexpectedly gets interrupted by circumstances completely out of your control. Whether you were prepared and saw it coming or you didn't, what you do next will define your future. You can choose to let circumstances either derail you into despair, guilt, condemnation and keep you searching for answers to questions you cannot solve, or you can choose to let it launch you into your God-given purpose. It's up to you.

In my case, the disruption in my life and business was totally unexpected, and I was not at all prepared for it. Ultimately, I found myself at a fork in the road, forced to make some of the best decisions in my life which equipped me to help business owners all over the world like myself. It is what drives me to help other leaders, professionals and entrepreneurs find the success they long to achieve.

So, I want to share a bit of my story with you before we get into the details of business success. **Why?** Because at the root of your success, you have a reason, a need, a determination that drives you to succeed. You have to know—really know—why you are doing what you are doing and **why** you will not give up on your dreams.

TURNED UPSIDE DOWN

It was around seven o'clock on what I thought was just another, very normal Tuesday night. I usually stayed late at the office every Tuesday and Thursday evening to catch up on design work at the business my husband Bill and I owned. That night was no different than any other, until the phone rang.

"Hello," I said.

The unfamiliar voice on the other end of the line said, "Hello, is this Mrs. Bush?"

"Yes, it is. Can I help you?" I responded.

"Is this Margo Bush? And is your husband Bill Bush?" he said.

"Yes," I responded. "Who is this?"

"This is Captain Mark from the police department. I'm calling to see if you are about ready to come home, Mrs. Bush."

My heart began to pound. Why was the police department calling me? "Yes, I am," I said. "Are Casey and Bill all right?" Casey was my teenage son, and Bill my husband, and I immediately wanted to know that they were safe.

"Well, that is what we want to talk about," Captain Mark said. "Please make your way home. Don't rush. We'll be here when you arrive. Please drive carefully." Click! The call abruptly ended with no explanation.

Anxious and confused, I ran around our 4,200 square foot publishing and printing facility, turning off lights, making sure doors were locked, and heading outside to the car. My hands were shaking so much that I could hardly get the key in to lock my office door. My twenty-minute drive home was… Well, you can only imagine. The scenes rapidly firing off in my head were not only crazy but unfamiliar. What in the world could have happened? Drugs, fighting, a break-in, theft?

When I pulled into our neighborhood, there were so many emergency vehicles with lights flashing, it looked like our neighborhood was lit up for Christmas in September. They were lined up all down the street. As I approached, I could see there was nowhere in front of my home to park, so I pulled into a neighbor's driveway. A police officer met me as I exited my car, as other officers formed a gauntlet up to our front door. I can only assume that the officer greeting me was Captain Mark. I didn't even ask who he was, because I was so unsettled.

Again, I was asked, "Are you Mrs. Bush, Billy Joe Bush's wife?"

"Yes!" I responded as the officer escorted me across the yard, up the steps to our front door and into the house. As I looked around for a familiar face, I saw my family, Bill's brothers and our oldest son, Adam, all standing against the living room wall. *That's odd*, I thought.

Where is Bill? I thought, as an officer led me into the living room to have a seat on the couch. Just then, Casey stepped out from the kitchen to join me as a Chaplain pulled up a chair to face me. What could have happened? I looked to Casey for answers; the tears pouring out of his bloodshot eyes spoke volumes. Something bad had really happened. But what? I glanced back at the Chaplain, with my heart pounding so hard I could almost hear it. Even now as I write this section of my story, some of those same feelings I felt that unexpected night begin to fill my eyes with tears and make my heart race. Nothing could have prepared me for what was about to come.

"Mrs. Bush," the Chaplain said in a gentle voice, "your husband is dead."

"That's not possible," I responded, in a controlled, calm statement. "I was just with Bill last night, and he was fine." I turned to look at Casey, he nodded his head, confirming a yes. I then looked over my shoulder to the right, scanning the wall as I looked for Adam. He also nodded his head, acknowledging his dad had died.

It's not always easy to move past such unexpected tragedy. I felt like my life, the life I shared with Bill, and my future was being ripped away from me. My heart was broken; it felt like it had been sliced open with a butcher knife, laying raw and exposed on a cement sidewalk. I got married when I was just twenty years old, straight out of my parents' home. Adam was a honeymoon baby, so I really never knew what it was like to live alone or solely support myself. Bill was an exceptional husband and father, so there were no regrets in my life. We worked together most of our married life, traveled the world speaking, enjoyed life together, and he always made sure I knew I was the center of his universe.

I had an overwhelming flood of emotions flowing through my mind and body. As the EMTs carried my husband's body out to the ambulance, I was escorted to the car where it seemed I was leaving one life behind and supposed to find a new life overnight. In that one very short moment in time when I heard those words, "Your husband is dead," my past, present and future flashed before my eyes. Life had been interrupted and there was no forewarning. My past was now cherished memories that Bill and I had made together with our children, our church and with each other. My future, as we looked forward to the new families our children would one day build—he would not be here to see that. And now my present was uncertain and unfamiliar. There were so many questions and few answers. The sorrow was so large and the grief so deep that it hurt to breathe.

"How can this be happening?" I thought. "I'm only in my forties and I'm a widow. This is just all very wrong."

What now? What was I going to do? Everything had changed and life looked very different now, and yet I didn't even know what that meant either. I did know one thing: my life insurance policy was sitting on my desk in my office, unsigned. Yes, you heard me—unsigned. Bill had told me several times to sign it, and I hadn't gotten around to it yet.

UNFINISHED BUSINESS

After the funeral was over and everyone went home to continue their lives, reality set in quickly. I was now faced for the first time in my life with the question of how to live life alone, work and make money.

I should have been more prepared for his loss, but I wasn't. As a result, the road ahead would be very rocky and filled with uncertainty, and I knew it.

Questions pounded at me: What was I supposed to do now? What was I to do with the publishing company we owned? What was my purpose? Was it the same as it had always been? Was it different now that Bill was gone?

After a few weeks, I began to show up at the office. Though we had a small staff, they now looked to me for direction. I had always been second in command and I liked it that way. That had been my role for twenty-eight years. Now, even though I was scared and grieving, I had also become the CEO of our book publishing company. More than ever before, the business would need to grow if I was going to support myself and my teenage son.

The problem was, I didn't know how to make money or create real increase in a business. I was grieving and seeking desperately for direction. Yet I had no other choice but to try and find my path and purpose in the middle of all this chaos. My greatest fear was that I would fail, that I would not be able to take care of myself, and that I would end up living under a bridge with a teenager, unable to properly provide for his future and mine. This possible future really became my *greatest* motivation to find a way to succeed.

DIGGING DEEP

Years ago, I heard a story about a group of people traveling on a routine air flight when unexpected turbulence occurred, and their plane went down on a remote island somewhere in the middle of the South China Sea. The passengers survived the emergency landing, but all communication had been lost with the mainland airport towers. They were cut off.

As each passenger made their way out of the plane, they began to assess their devastating situation. It became clear that they were lost and without hope of ever being found. You can only imagine the fear and despair that began to set in as each passenger one-by-one expressed their fears that they would never see their families again or be found and rescued.

At that moment, one passenger stepped up with a plan. You know, you never have to look hard for a true leader. They will always migrate to the top and step out of the crowd. You just can't keep them down. They naturally step up and begin to lead the way. They may not always do it right, they may not always have the solution just perfect, but they will try hard and you will rarely ever have to motivate them. They have a winning fight inside them, like a candle on a hill that can't be put out. They rise to the challenge every time, regardless of the risk it takes.

We will call this leader Edward. Edward did his best to calm the passengers and then asked each one to go and get their luggage out of the plane. He instructed them to lay each piece of luggage open on the ground, in an orderly fashion next to each other. Then Edward challenged each person to go through their belongings one piece at a time to find any tools, medical supplies, food and other items that could possibly be used for survival.

Each passenger gathered their belongings as Edward had instructed them and put each item in the appropriate pile labeled accordingly. Slowly, the stacks began to grow as they added each item. After combining the items they had pulled out of their luggage, these travelers discovered something very surprising. Together, they had enough items to not only survive, but to thrive. With proper, disciplined mastery of their situation, they could actually build a future on that island together, whether they were ever found or not, because of what they had all brought along on their journey.

> A woman is like a tea bag; you never know how strong it is until it's in hot water.
> —ELEANOR ROOSEVELT, former first lady of the U.S.

This is where I found myself after my husband died—it was like crash-landing on an island in the middle of nowhere, and having to figure out how to survive. I had two choices in my desperate situation. I could either dig deep into my toolbox and learn how to grow the business I had been left, or I could go to work nine-to-five for minimum wage.

First, I had always been in control of my own hours, and didn't like the idea of having to report to someone else nine-to-five. Second, I knew that when you work for someone else, you work to fulfill their dreams and visions, not yours. When you are an employee, you are a commodity, and if someone comes along who is better than you for half the price, it is better for the company to hire that person and let you go. This decision is not personal; it is just business.

I also knew that the wealthiest people on earth are those who create their own wealth through entrepreneurship. This, then, was my vision, my new purpose in life. I had to find the courage to walk this new road of entrepreneurship alone. This time, my life and business would be different, and nothing about it would feel the same.

FACING CHALLENGES

Sometimes, we don't realize what we are capable of achieving until we're faced with circumstances that force us to dig deep and do more than we ever thought possible.

Perhaps you can relate to this. It may be that you are dealing with a major personal loss, as I did. Maybe you've had a business fail already, or you've started a business but can't seem to grow it. You might have declared bankruptcy. Or perhaps you have lost a job and are struggling to find another way to bring in income.

One of the most difficult things to face in life and business is to feel like you have no real, marketable skills—even after years of working hard. Many of the people I coach have lost a job they loved. After years of commitment to an organization, they have suddenly been replaced by someone younger who is willing to work for half the salary. All that experience they gained, all the skills they brought to the table, and for what? It's a painful, discouraging position to be in.

Believe me, I know what that feels like, because I went through it too. After my husband's untimely death, I was lost as to what to do, especially when it came to business. At the very least, I needed a job to pay bills. But I didn't even have a resume. Serving as a pastor's wife is a position that requires a tremendous amount of skills—but it's not an actual job title, and it can't be verified in a job interview. It put me at a disadvantage in terms of job seeking, even with all the experience and skills I had.

By the time I was twenty-one, Bill and I had our first little boy and we were all traveling the world together. We were speaking at conventions throughout the U.S., traveling with major ministries while running our own business and non-profit organization. After a few years, we began pastoring a struggling church of about twenty that soon went to ten, but eventually grew successfully to over eight hundred people in a small town of less than twenty thousand. Eventually we built a building. I built a thriving music and fine arts department, managed a large volunteer staff, and together we counseled hundreds of people each year.

I had always worked hard, but in partnership with my spouse. We learned to work very well together, respecting one another's gifts and talents, and had fun building our future. But now, he was gone. He was no longer living on this planet and I had no resume. The one person who could vouch for my abilities or my work ethic didn't have an address or a phone number anyone could contact.

Bill and I were very good at building and growing successful churches, but how did that translate into running a business that would support the family? I wasn't sure if I had the answers I needed to build a strong, thriving business. I look back now and realize I had many of the tools needed to begin a new life. I had more experience in business-related skills than a lot of people have in an entire lifetime due to the work and people I managed in my earlier days. But I didn't know it then. I didn't know what I had or how to leverage it. I didn't know the value of *me*.

Find your courage, even when life's disruptions have hit hard. And it will not always be easy. But I encourage you to step back, look at the bigger picture of your life, and think about how much you've accomplished, what you've learned, and what tools you really have at your disposal. It is probably a longer list than you think.

TAKE THE NEXT STEP

One of the greatest choices we can make in life is to evaluate where we are right now and ask, "Is what I am doing working? Am I at the place I want to be in my life, my career and my finances? What does my financial future look like? Does my future look brighter than my past?"

If the answers to these questions is *no*, then you have the power to change that. When you decide to make changes, it puts you on an open road to fulfilling your greatest destiny. It's time to seek out information, knock continuously, and ask important questions that will move the needle in your quest for success. Take charge of what is not working, take ownership and have the courage to move forward.

No matter what you are facing right now, no matter what isn't working, I want to encourage you to keep pursuing your destiny. Your greatest opportunities are ahead of you, and there is a bright future in front of you as you overcome doubts and embrace the truth that you were born for more. It will take courage, but you can do it. It starts with taking that next step.

In my own life and career, success has come not by leaps or jumps, but one step at a time. I usually see the first step to take, and then once I take that step, I see the next step. I've had really big things happen in my career that were so unexpected. Many of these things would never have happened if I hadn't taken that first step, by faith, even though I could not see what was ahead of me.

Sometimes you just have to do life afraid, uncomfortable, and find the faith inside yourself to smother out the fear. You won't always see the full distance of the road ahead—especially when it comes to business. You won't always see what's over the hill or around the corner, especially when you're first starting out. But most of the time, you can see the next step.

In gaining your own success, you'll see the beginning and the end, but the middle will be fuzzy. In the middle, you'll need to find the education you need to clear up the fog. You will continually refine your skills, tweak your approach, and move into new positions as you climb the ladder of successful entrepreneurship. Your practice ground is in between the beginning and the end. You're not always going to get it right.

The fear of not knowing what comes next will try to stop you from taking the next step. Don't talk yourself out of what's possible and certainly don't let anyone else do so. Your success is waiting on the other side of that fear you're battling.

Just taking the next step will take you farther down the road than you are right now. And you'll see more than before you took the step. Be sure to do your homework, calculate the risk, test the waters and then take the step. But for heaven's sake, don't just stand there doing nothing, because doing nothing produces nothing.

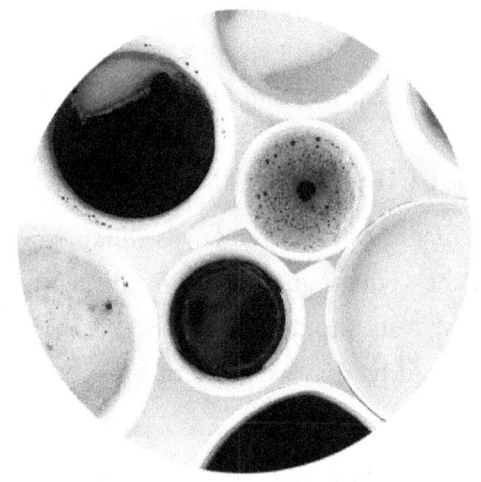

CHAPTER THREE

Opportunity Awaits

Don't limit yourself.
You can go as far as your mind lets you.
—MARY KAY ASH, founder of Mary Kay Cosmetics

Throughout history, we have heard the stories of extraordinary entrepreneurs who have challenged us to do more, go farther, and dream bigger. These people have changed our lives, created successful businesses, achieved great things, and inspired us to follow our dreams. In these next few pages, I want us to take a look into the lives of a few extraordinary people who lived intentionally, and turned their dreams into reality. Some have been in the news, many in our history books. Their stories give us hope, inspiration, faith, and the courage to step out beyond our fears to do more—in business and in life.

PURSUING OUR PURPOSE

Let's take a look first at Mother Teresa, a woman who made a lifelong commitment to the saving and comfort of humanity worldwide. She said, "Our deepest fears should not be that we are inadequate. Our deepest regrets should be that we go to our graves not doing what we were put on this earth to do."

It could not have been easy to minister to hurting humanity in what is the world's largest slum, Calcutta, a place of great poverty. Time and time again, she had obstacles to overcome. Mother Teresa met those challenges one day at a time, because she knew what she was put here to do. She reached into one wounded life at a time and changed the world as she practiced a lifetime of caring for people. She decided to step into the space of life that had her name on it. She found her purpose, her calling, and took one step at a time to fulfill what she dreamed of doing.

If we only realized, as Mother Teresa apparently did, that we are powerful beyond measure! We would see that we have the same opportunities as so many extraordinary people who surround us have had. Opportunities surround you every day, but you will have to live life intentionally, determined to pursue your dream, if you're going to recognize those opportunities when they come along.

When you see an opportunity, it is my advice to take action. Afraid or not, take action. The first step will always be the hardest, and you might have to do it in spite of worries, insecurities, or the voice of your own inner critic. But once you take that first step, your path will become clearer as you go along. You'll find your success; it is waiting for you, beyond the fear.

RAISING THE BAR ON SUCCESS

Mary Kay Ash was a woman who led a movement that has now lasted for more than five decades. Against all odds, against disappointments, she found her own unique voice and ultimately her lifelong purpose; and it all happened *after retirement*. When most people were finishing their career, she began a new chapter in her life that has empowered millions of women to succeed.

As a professional sales executive turned entrepreneur, she began her first business from a tiny store in Dallas, Texas, with five products and a big dream. Her dream was to inspire women to take charge of their own destiny and transform their lives. In doing so, she helped women worldwide achieve the American dream to create success.

Today, with more than three million Independent Beauty Consultants, Mary Kay offers more than two hundred premium products in more than thirty-five countries around the world. For fifty years, Mary Kay has helped women discover a new passion, a new purpose, at any age and any stage in life. Her success reminds us all of what we can become when we are given the power to achieve it. And she did this all after retirement

DON'T HOLD BACK

Like Mary Kay, we all have dreams, whether it is for our business or for some other area of our life. But often, we limit ourselves before we can truly achieve those dreams. "Who am I to write a bestselling book?" we ask. "Who am I to become the next president or CFO of a great company? Who am I to invent the next medical breakthrough?"

Actually, who are you not? You are more capable of success than you may realize. Why do we hold back?

I have met a lot of brilliant men and women in my publishing, pastoring and business consulting career. Are they all that different from you and me? After all, we all came into this world the same way. We all come out fighting for that next breath to survive. We were not born to fail. Each one of us was born with our own desires and passions to fulfill. Don't talk yourself out of it—and certainly don't let anyone else do so.

We all have our name on a piece of life that we are to occupy. I like to say it like this: when we buy land or a house, we take up that space on the planet. We purchase it. It is now ours to do with as we choose. We can plant trees, build a garden, raise chickens, build a barn or build a house, because we own that space.

It is this way with our purpose in life, our dreams, and our careers. We each have a part to play in this symphony called life. How much a part of the music you want to play is up to you. It is no one else's job to make you play. If you want to play small, you can. If you want to play big, you can. If you want to be good at it, then you must put in the practice time. Own your space!

EMPOWERED TO ACHIEVE

Mary Pickford became the most powerful woman who has ever worked in Hollywood. As a child in the early 1900s, Pickford, along with her mother and two younger siblings, toured the United States by rail, performing in third-rate companies and plays. After six impoverished years of acting, a fourteen-year-old Pickford allowed herself one more summer to attempt to land a leading role on Broadway, planning to quit if she failed.

She never had to follow through with that plan, because she finally landed a supporting role in a 1907 Broadway play, *The Warrens of Virginia*. After completing the Broadway run and touring the play, Pickford broke into feature films.

> Anything is possible, if you believe it is possible.
>
> —*Alice Through the Looking Glass, 2016 film*

An astute businesswoman, Pickford became her own producer within three years. In the traditionally male-dominated world of filmmaking, she took charge of her own destiny. With a strong hands-on approach, she handled every aspect of the making of her films, from hiring talent and crew to overseeing the script, the shooting and the editing, to managing the final release and promotion of each project.

After her refusal to participate in block-booking, the widespread industry practice of forcing an exhibitor to show a bad film of the studio's choosing, Pickford single-handedly, through a special distribution unit called Artcraft, began producing her own films, establishing The Mary Pickford Corporation and later becoming co-founder of United Artists. In consideration of her contributions to American cinema, the American Film Institute named Pickford as one of the greatest female stars of all time.

PUT IN THE TIME

To take charge of your destiny at a level that Pickford achieved, you can't hold back. You have to put in the time and discipline it takes to reach mastery of your craft—and you can expect the commitment to be significant. Worth it, but significant.

In college, I was a music and theater major. Some things about music and theater performance came naturally for me. Other parts were hard, uncomfortable, and required a lot of practice time. The time you put into something—such as your business—is crucial to your success.

For example, I really wanted to learn how to play the piano and perform better when I was forty, so I went back to college to get my theater and music performance degree. At that point in my life, I had been playing music on stage for more than fifteen years, yet I was never as good as I wanted to be. Even in college, I wouldn't put in the hours it took to accomplish top performance status. Playing piano at that level was difficult and required more effort than I was willing to put in.

It can be this way for us and our businesses too. If you want to do better, you've got to put in the time to practice and learn business principles. This is the only way you develop the disciplined mastery required to achieve the long-term success you desire. I started my first business when I was nineteen. I look back now and realize it was practice ground. My second business was good, but not great. I sold it for much less than I put into it. But it, too, was a practice ground for what I am doing today.

Over the years, I have chosen to put more practice time into my business and speaking than I put into my piano playing. As a result, I've been speaking professionally for years now, and I only play the piano for pleasure. We accomplish what we put in the time to accomplish. It's up to us to choose it.

PIONEERING

Amelia Mary Earhart, born July 24, 1897, and disappearing July 2, 1937, was an American aviation pioneer and author. Earhart was the first female aviator to fly solo across the Atlantic Ocean, an accomplishment for which she received the U.S. Distinguished Flying Cross. Over the course of her career, she won several awards, wrote best-selling books about her flying experiences, and helped establish The Ninety-Nines, an organization for female pilots. Earhart joined the Purdue University aviation department in 1935 as a visiting faculty member to counsel women on their careers and help inspire others with her love for aviation.

Although Earhart had gained fame for her first transatlantic flight in 1928, which was in the company of others who piloted the plane, she decided to set her own record by setting off on her first long solo flight that same year, just as her name was coming into the national spotlight. By successfully making this trip in August 1928, Earhart became the first woman to fly solo across the North American continent and back.

Several years later, during an attempt to fly around the world in 1937, Earhart disappeared over the central Pacific Ocean near Howland Island. Because of Earhart's extraordinary life and career, the fascination people have with her disappearance continues to this day.

Earhart pushed the boundaries of what was considered possible, breaking new ground in the process. Just as people like the Wright Brothers, she pushed the limits. Just as there were no personal computers before Steve Jobs and Bill Gates came along, there were no female aviators before Earhart. She refused to let that stop her.

We can become so boxed into our own little world that it is hard to step out of the box and do something bigger than we've ever seen anyone do before. Earhart watched others fly, learned what to do, and then achieved what no woman had achieved before because she had the determination and boldness to dream—and then put action to that dream.

PERSISTENCE PAYS OFF

The life of Helen Beatrix Potter, an English author and illustrator best known for her imaginative children's books featuring animals such as those in *The Tale of Peter Rabbit*, is an inspiration to all writers who have a story that needs to be told. Because of her passion to write and illustrate, children all over the world are still learning about life through her characters.

The Tale of Peter Rabbit became one of the most famous illustrated children's books ever written and the basis of Potter's future career as a writer, artist, and storyteller. Because of her accomplishments, it may appear that success came easily for her. But *The Tale of Peter Rabbit* was initially rejected by publishers because Potter was a woman and her story was what someone at the time called a "silly tale."

But one year later, after much persuasion and persistence, Potter convinced a publisher to reconsider her work. Eager to compete in the booming small format children's book market, the publisher accepted what the company called the "bunny book." On October 2, 1902, *The Tale of Peter Rabbit* was published widely and became an immediate success. Throughout her career, Helen eventually published over twenty-three books.

> You had a purpose before anyone had an opinion.
> —ZIG ZIGLAR, best-selling author of See You at the Top

Helen Beatrix Potter was not only persistent; she became a savvy businesswoman. Not just content with writing books, she created and patented a Peter Rabbit doll and other merchandise over the years—what is known today as spin-off materials—such as painting books, board games, wallpaper, figurines, baby blankets and china tea sets. This meant that the successful sales of these items provided a hefty independent income for Potter well after the book was published. By creating a continual source of income at a time when her funny little book seemed insignificant and was looked upon at first as silly, she provided herself a lasting income long after the initial work was completed.

Peter Rabbit and the merchandise built around the book published provided Helen financial security way beyond that first book. This is considered passive, residual income. Potter became a very rich woman because she considered a market and built it.

Residual income is the amount of net income generated beyond the initial expense of an item produced or bought, the level of income that an individual has after the deduction of all personal debts and expenses have been paid. Passive income is the profit made from a particular item, such as rental property that is owned by investors who are not actively involved in managing the property. Another example is a dividend-producing stock that pays an annual percentage. While an investor must purchase the stock to realize the passive income, no other effort or work is required beyond the initial investment.

The attraction of establishing some sort of method for earning passive income is that it frees an individual to do other things with their time besides work. If the passive income is big enough, then someone can live off of that investment for a very long time, sometimes a lifetime.

Passive income offers increasing levels of financial security. Although you might take a risk when first establishing the mechanism for passive income, if it proves to be a steady flow, it offers great security because it's not connected to your time.

PURSUING PURPOSE

If you are a follower of ancient scripture, there is a businesswoman who I particularly enjoy studying. She stands out among all the rest—Lydia of Thyatira. She is most commonly known by historians and those who study theology as The Woman of Purple.

> A woman named Lydia, a dealer in purple cloth from
> the city of Thyatira, was listening.
> —The Book of Acts, chapter 16

Lydia was a well-to-do businesswoman who made a purple dye in Thyatira, a city southeast of Pergamum and approximately forty miles inland, across the Aegean Sea from Athens. Famous for all its dyes, Thyatira was especially well-known for its unique purple, which was prized by the Romans. Lydia traveled across the oceans, bringing rolls of dyed cloth to sell, unaware she would meet a man named Paul. She ended up assisting him in the startup of an influential church at Philippi.

Why did she come just at that time? How did she happen to be in Philippi? Why not Neapolis? Why not press on to Athens? Why not sell her cloth over in Corinth? Whatever reason she might have given for her choice, there was one cause, of which she was unaware, which shaped the rest of her life and her destiny, bringing her to Philippi at this particular time to meet Paul and help him start the Philippian church. It never entered Lydia's mind when she left Thyatira with her purple bales that she was following a thread that would bring her to her greater purpose.

What an odd thing that this entrepreneurial woman of Thyatira needed to go to Philippi, and Paul needed to go to Philippi at the same time. She was unaware that the journey she was about to take when she left Thyatira was in pursuit of her purpose. If we knew all the circumstances in her life that led her to that point, no doubt we would be amazed. If we look closely at our own lifelong journey, we would see a similar thread of purpose and be amazed at the wisdom of it.

I wonder if there are a number of provenances we have all had in our lives that we overlooked—places we have traveled to, people we have met, unaware of the importance they would have in our stories. Your journey has brought you to this place, at this time, to meet a certain person or friend in order to fulfill your dreams. You may yet be unaware of this providential guidance, but it is there, because you have a purpose. And all of the universe will move to fulfill it if you lean into the process and just trust.

EVERYONE HAS A STORY

My own story, which I've shared with you, is of finding my own destiny in entrepreneurship after a devastating personal loss. I felt a bit like the widow woman in the scriptures who only had a few pots of oil. After a divine encounter with the prophet, she ended up in the oil business.

> Faith sees the invisible, believes the unbelievable,
> and receives the impossible.
> —CORRIE TEN BOOM, author of The Hiding Place

When my husband died, I was under a lot of pressure to run a successful business and support my family properly. Worst of all, the voice of fear taunted me continually. The image of living under a bridge with a teenager, unable to build anything for the future, spoke to me in a loud strong voice. At that point, my *why*—my purpose—became greater than my fears. This pushed me forward and I began to lean into my true destiny.

Instead of allowing your fears to kill your dreams, use your fears to fuel them. I'm proclaiming to you today in a strong voice of encouragement, You got this! You can and will see your greatest days ahead. With a little bit of education, a great work ethic and a lot of hope, you can see your dream of successful business ownership. It was the fight to win which gave me purpose again, and purpose fueled my pursuit to succeed. Passion breeds purpose, and purpose fuels pursuit. I believe your best days are ahead.

Today, I own three businesses and have coached hundreds of business owners from startups to million-dollar entities nationwide. We have helped more than one hundred authors get published and sold more than 100,000 books worldwide. And I am not nearly done yet or helped the number of people that we want to reach.

My goal is to empower one million business owners through better avenues of education, entrepreneurial training, support, and philanthropy.

For me, someone took my hand when I needed education, training and support. And now, I am doing the same for others. Dreams are possible, and honest prayers never go unheard. We can all help each other be successful.

CHAPTER FOUR

The Art of People

Start with good people, lay out the rules, communicate well, motivate and reward them. If you do all those things effectively, you can't miss.
—LEE IACOCCA, American automobile executive

One thing I've learned over the years is that there are definitely two sides to success.

The first is the journey we're on as human beings—what we learn about life and work, the experiences we have, the people we meet, the impact we make on humanity. The journey you are on *in life* is a valuable one, and I definitely believe we all have a purpose we are to fulfill while on this earth—the lives we are to impact and the people who are to impact our lives. A part of that journey is the career(s) we choose, and the relationships we become involved in are an important piece of fulfilling our divine destiny. Whether you know what your purpose is or not, we all have one.

But the journey, by itself alone, does not guarantee success. For the most part, most people have worked very hard to create a good life and financial security. But still through it all, many people still find themselves coming up short each month, each year. Creating success and building a good business aren't just about how hard you work or even about just showing up each day. If you don't set a destination point of profitability, then all of the good intentions in the world won't create the success you are looking for. Profitable businesses stay out of the red and remain in the black. They have more coming in than going out, a lot more. This is simply a fact; it's all in the *math*, nothing more, nothing less.

The journey we're on and the keys to success in business often seem to get confused. In fact, I meet people all the time who have had such amazing life journeys to where they are today—so amazing that I've been inclined to stay up half the night, enthralled, hanging on their every word and waiting with anticipation for the next twist or turn. We're talking *blockbuster* stuff here. They've been everywhere, done so much, and it is compelling to listen to their stories. I love a great story!

But before the night is over, I realize that the amazing person sitting in front of me doesn't have *anything* financially to show for it. They could be one of the most interesting people on the planet, yet they have nothing in their bank account, and their life and business are struggling to the point they do not know what they are going to do next if they don't see a miracle by the end of the month. They have very little to show for all they've experienced in life. They have way too much credit card debt, so much that it keeps them up at night. They have a loan on their car that is upside down, and they are hoping they can meet payroll by the end of the month.

The mistake most small business owners make is that they believe if they just stay on the road long enough, and gain enough experience, they will somehow, some way earn the right to make a lot of money and gain success. They believe that through the process of osmosis, their journey will give them the proper information and alliances needed to make them financially secure. While this may have happened to some, it simply isn't the norm, at least for the vast majority of people. And of course, there are those times in life that unexpected things happen that somehow cause us to pull it all together and make it through. I have lived that life, and it is no fun wondering, hoping, guessing, praying for a miracle that comes just in the nick of time. Who wants to live like that? I don't, and for years I did, as a business owner just making it barely through that month. It's hard, exhausting and needless to say, challenging. It eventually becomes discouraging. Do you agree with all of that?

I'm here to tell you: A person's journey, no matter how amazing it is or how long it lasts, has absolutely nothing to do with their ability to make money. Just because you've had an incredible journey that may have spanned decades doesn't mean we've figured out how to translate those experiences into dollars and cents.

You've got to learn how to make money. I mean, the kind of money deserving of, and equal to, the journey you have had. If you take a million-dollar journey and only learn how to master twenty thousand dollars a year, this would be a great injustice to both you and your journey

SALES AND PEOPLE

A man once said to me, "Building a business is simple; I'm not saying it is easy, but it is simple." It basically boils down to a simple idea: You must learn to sell what you have produced. Whether it is a service or a product, you must provide the value and opportunity to enough people for them to experience what you have to sell, and then convince them to buy it (and keep buying). That means educating yourself as a business owner, and then mastering the ability to bring your product to market.

To be successful in business, we must first understand ourselves, who we are personally as business owners, and frankly, as human beings. You need to know who you are, how you are most comfortable working, your strengths, weaknesses and the fears you need to overcome. Just as importantly, you need to understand the people who need your product and the market you want to reach. The art of people has become one of the most interesting segments of business for me, more than almost anything else I do.

I really like studying the buying power of groups of people. This is very important when you want to grow and market your business. For most of us, we have only thought of sales as the car salesman who chases us down on the parking lot as we drive through looking at new cars. You know, that one you avoid eye contact with while they are walking towards you, and then when you stop for just a moment not to hit a pedestrian, he/she knocks on your window. Sales is not a hit and run. Sales is a relationship built between you, your company and the customer. Customers are the heartbeat of any profitable organization, and they deserve your time and attention.

Building relationships with your customers and providing them a product they deserve, your product, is one of the greatest opportunities we have as a company. The next time you think of sales, think of it as serving people and building relationships. Directly or indirectly, that is what you are doing. Then be consistent to provide a product or service that meets their expectations over and over again. If you can do this, you will have a customer for life.

I was never a natural at sales. In fact, for many years, our business broke just a little over even most of the time. We had good cash flow, but that doesn't add up to a lifestyle of living great. It adds up to working hard like crazy to pay bills, but not being able to go on vacation and rest, because you know when you get back, you will pay for being gone and have to work longer, harder hours to catch back up and make end-of-the-month payroll.

Great sales hinge on making what you're selling important enough to people that they want it, they want it from you and they want to keep coming back and buying from you. That begins with understanding people and why they buy what they buy. I know there are a lot of personality tests out there you can take, and many of us have done several of them throughout our careers. I have always been in the people business. I started out my career caring for people in the hospital, then for more than twenty-five years I was a pastor's wife. I will boil it down for you here what I have done to make it quick and easy to identify people and their core personalities. I do not write personality tests, so this is in no way diving deep into the psychology or science of people. Over my more than 30 years of working with people in all different areas of life, this has served me as a quick reference. What works for me is that I have narrowed it down to four core personality types—what I'll refer here to as the aggressor, the analyst, the expressive, and the giver.

Once you start to really understand these different personalities, I believe you'll start to find it much easier to pinpoint the different people you impact, sell to, and interact with daily. Building teams in your business will become much easier for you because you'll understand the people around you, their strengths, weaknesses and how you affect them, as much as how they affect you. This won't work if you are convinced everyone should adapt to you and you don't want to change or be open to seeing your own personal weaknesses as an opportunity to grow beyond where you are today.

Knowing personalities will help you understand your partner(s), coworker(s), employee(s), clients, potential customers, and vendors. If you learn these four core principles about people and how they want to be approached and worked with, you can build a killer team and create real profits. You will add true value when dealing with potential customers and win the deal on their terms. Everyone wins, and success begins to happen.

And even more importantly, it will help you realize your own personality and how it works. Once you know how *you* work, you'll know some crucial things about how to make your business more successful than ever before. As you read ahead, see if you can identify your own personality, and think about the people you interact with regularly. Can you identify them as well?

THE AGGRESSOR

The Aggressor likes to be in charge and is very goal-oriented. This personality type often gravitates toward careers where they are in control and can accomplish clear goals. You'll find Aggressors in roles such as business owners, corporate CEOs, independent consultants, stockbrokers, or drill sergeants. Some examples of famous Aggressors include Alexander the Great, Donald Trump, Oprah Winfrey, Rudy Giuliani, and Colin Powell.

If you look at an Aggressor, you'll notice they display most, or all, of these characteristics: They are results-oriented, bottom-line focused, and driven by accomplishment. They can be highly competitive, and they like getting things done and making things happen. Often, they can seem impersonal or perhaps emotionless (though that's not necessarily the case). They enjoy being in control, which means they not only readily disclose their often high expectations, but they can be opinionated, even impatient. They may have poor listening skills because they are focused on their goals and determined to get things accomplished. They're time conscious. And they are risk takers.

You'll see their personality not just in behavior but in their physical attributes too. Their clothing and belongings are usually bold, dominant and striking. What they display in their office is all about goals and achievement. You won't generally see a jar of candy, family photos or personal mementos on the desk of the Aggressive professional. Instead, their office décor suggests power with awards and honors often displayed. The seating is formal.

RELATING TO THE AGGRESSOR

To make a more dynamic connection with the Aggressive client, get to the point as quickly as possible. Offer concise explanations and focus on the outcome rather than the process. This individual wants to know the bottom line: "How is this going to benefit me? What's it going to cost me? How much money will we make or save? When will this project be completed?"

Avoid personal issues, especially theirs. They do not appreciate you getting too close. Suggest ideas for business strategies instead. Do not use pointless humor or engage in small talk, like "How was your weekend?" They're not interested in sharing that.

Instead, stay focused on the topic at hand. Aggressors do not want to know the long process you used to arrive at your own conclusion. Rather than going into great detail, sum up the situation, and conclude with a call for action — one that they can delegate.

When looking for ways to reach the Aggressor customer, consider promoting speedy service, bottom-line savings, and solid, no-hassle guarantees.

THE ANALYST

The Analyst is very analytical and thorough. This individual tends to get caught up in the process rather than focus on the outcome. He or she is usually introverted and reserved. You'll find Analyst people in careers where analysis and detail-oriented work is key, such as accounting, computer programming, engineering, architecture, systems analysis, dentistry, and other technical or hard-science professions.

Examples are Albert Einstein, Steven Hawking, Ralph Nader and Bill Gates.

Among the characteristics of a typical Analyst, you'll see that they are good at problem solving and working at solitary tasks. They're logical and methodical in their work. As analytical introverts, they usually learn best by reading. They're reserved, self-contained, reliable, and conscious of time. They're usually good with finances, where their analytical eye for detail is advantageous. Because they are so analytical, they're often slower to make decisions than the Aggressor. They avoid taking risks, and they hate to be wrong.

You'll recognize their personality in their possessions too. Their clothing tends to be conservative, as they are not out to make any fashion statements. Do not expect to find much in the way of personal expressions, photos or decorative touches in their office. Their desk might be covered with neat piles of charts and graphs. Where is the chair for the visitor placed? The question is not where, but whether there is a chair at all. This type of personality is task-oriented and focused on work, not on entertaining visitors to the office.

RELATING TO THE ANALYST

As you interact with the Analyst, you will find these types of purchasers or clients are slower to part with their money and make decisions if you do not give them a detailed process of your product or service. They require a great deal of information with statistics to accept a claim.

In addition, be formal and logical. Normally, Analysts do not welcome physical contact unless they invite it, so limit such contact to handshakes.

The Analyst hears you best when you use terms such as precise, logical, tested, and proven. As you speak with them, focus on key points such as product ratings, consumer reviews, testimonials and other solid studies. These elements will help speed up their decision-making process.

THE EXPRESSIVE

Expressives are the most personable and outgoing of all personality types. (I'm one!) As the name implies, they are happiest and most productive when they can embrace their jobs with passion and excitement. They do not mind being in the spotlight, and they enjoy contact with others. You'll find them in careers that thrive on interaction with others and being the center of attention, such as sales, trial law, public relations, and acting. One of my majors was music and theater; does that tell you anything about me? The best examples of Expressives are Kelly Clarkson, Blake Shelton, Kathie Lee Gifford and Jimmy Fallon.

Every company will thrive with Expressives on their staff. They are passionate and will become passionate about your business if you treat them right. They are high spirited and, if given the tools, will grow with you. The challenges for a CEO who is an Aggressor or Analyst is that Expressives need affirmation. That will take you a long way in getting the most out of a great personality. Expressives can become great CEOs if they recognize this about themselves, embrace it, and grow in the areas they are weak in, like processes. The solution: get a partner who is an Analyst or Aggressor to grow your company big.

When you meet an Expressive, you're likely to know it fast. They're creative, open and direct. Of course, they're people-oriented—which means they desire support from others, love attention, and enjoy being in the spotlight. They tend to make decisions quickly, because they are risk-takers and dream-chasers. Sometimes, they respond emotionally rather than logically to situations. They often generalize and exaggerate. And they get caught up in the moment, which means they're not particularly conscious of time.

These traits are evident in how they present themselves. They're not afraid to stand out, which means they enjoy clothing and possessions that are daring, loud, and attention-grabbing. Because they're focused on the moment, their office can be cluttered and disorganized. The walls are often covered with inspiring posters expressing motivational slogans. The arrangement will probably be open and friendly, with seating arranged so that people can talk easily.

RELATING TO THE EXPRESSIVE

Do not bore the Expressive with detailed facts and figures. They don't want to hear it. A straight lecture doesn't bear much fruit with these people. What they want to do is to experience the bells and whistles life has to offer. So, if you are selling to an enthusiastic Expressive person, then get them excited. Make your presentation even more fun than usual, and get the customer involved. They'll love it.

As you seek to persuade the Expressive, emphasize the bells and whistles. Use words that invite emotion and excitement, like *awesome, cool, best, sleek, latest* and *greatest*. Expressive clients will be drawn in by your passion, open body language, and enthusiastic voice tone. It is not what you say to these people; it's how you say it that matters.

If you are an Expressive and want to beat the odds to grow your business and make it all you want it to become, then pay attention to these areas above that would hinder growth in you and in your business. I started with paying attention to the small details, such as timing myself on how long I could sit and do a task without jumping up to get something. That was a shocker! I tamed that real quick. Instead of sitting for 15 minutes before I thought I needed to get up, now I can focus on a task for two hours at a time.

THE GIVER

The Giver is an individual who leads with emotion and is very instinctive and nurturing. They like people and want to make a difference. You'll find them in careers that tap into their nurturing nature, such as teachers, counselors, social workers, nursing, human resources and the ministry. They often occupy support roles rather than being the person in charge. Examples are Mother Teresa and former First Lady Barbara Bush.

Givers are typically dedicated workers and excellent team players. They often act as part of the support system of others in their careers and families. They're unassuming, open to others, reliable and loyal. They seek and enjoy close relationships. Givers usually avoid high-risk situations, meaning they can be hesitant to make decisions.

You'll notice that the Giver enjoys clothing and belongings that are unassuming too. They dress in outfits that are warm, inviting, calming, comfortable and relaxed. You're likely to see jars of candy, pictures of family and other personal items on the desk or walls. The atmosphere of their office is friendly. Often, the guest seating is more informal.

RELATING TO THE GIVER

While everyone needs some logic to persuade them, Givers do not need as much as the other personality types. What they do need more than most is the ability to relate to and trust you. You will convince these people more effectively with an informal, conversational approach or a group discussion where they do not feel singled out.

Givers thrive on contact. Close friends, long-term customers, loyal clients, and even friendly coworkers may—when appropriate—approach the Giver with warm handshakes, back patting, and even hugs. They love hugs. Graphs, charts, or long, involved discussions of statistics are appreciated but not as important as trust to a Giver. If they feel they can trust you, then it is a win!

When interacting with a Giver, realize that they will respond well to words such as *compatible, comfortable, warm, trust, participation, teamwork* and *user-friendly*. This individual will be comfortable opening his or her protective territory to allow you to stand closer. He or she responds well to food and gifts. A customer who is a Giver will also respond well to interest in his or her children or family. Ask about their family because it is most important to them, and at the core of everything they do.

CONTINUALLY LEARN AND GROW

I know there are several personality tests on the market today that are very good in guiding you personally and the people in your organization. Such tests can identify the best and most effective ways to work well with one another. However, I have found that being able to identify people in one of these four core personality types outlined in this chapter can help you better identify your customer more quickly, and how you should respond or approach the meeting you are about to enter into. Many times, I can compare the person sitting in the meeting with me by asking myself who are they most like, former first Lady Barbara Bush, Kelly Clarkson, Will Smith, Simon Cowell or Elon Musk?

We would like to think that life is all about us, how good we are at our job or how good we are at sales. The truth is that it is not about us at all; it is about the customer. How skillful are you at working with and talking to clients of all different personality types? It will always be much easier to relate to individuals who have the same or similar personality traits as you. But how good are you at working with people who are not like you? This is the true test of your sales skills.

I thought that I knew a lot about people because of my work in the ministry. I also thought learning the four core personality traits would be something I would use only once in a while. I have since realized that it is the foundation for everything I do in business, including how I hire, develop leaders, coach business owners, build teams, work with customers and build a relationship with my business partners.

Success in business depends on how good you are at understanding how people make a decision to purchase. You must know what is important to your customer, why they would want to buy from you, what benefits they are looking for in a product or service, and why they would want to purchase from you rather than your competitor.

I encourage you to take the time to study each personality in-depth.

CHAPTER FIVE

It's All In The Math

*Formal education will make you a living;
self-education will make you a fortune.*
—JIM ROHN, entrepreneur, author and motivational speaker

Because of the way we have been taught to do business and the way math works, it seems logical to expect a natural progression for making money and growing a business. For example, many people think, "Before I can earn a seven-figure income, I must first master the art of making a six-figure income." Or, "The only way I could ever make $500,000 is after I first make $100,000, then

$250,000, then $300,000 and so on. And then once I'm making that kind of money for a while, a long while, then I can think about getting into that million dollar range."

For many, this is the way we've been taught how business works. By thinking in these terms, we may feel like we are being logical and reasonable. You may have had parents who said, "Now, just don't get ahead of yourself. Take it slow." Have you ever heard the phrase, "Anything worth having is worth waiting for?" Why do people say that? Most of the time, it is because that's what they were taught, maybe by someone they trusted or were close to.

The *New York Times* best selling book, *Rich Dad, Poor Dad* provides insight into how our environment molds our thinking and even creates mental barriers that can pose a challenge to us. What we have heard throughout our lifetime, positive or negative, will eventually show up in the way we live our lives. Written by Robert T. Kiyosaki and Sharon Lechter, *Rich Dad, Poor Dad* is based on Kiyosaki's experience of living with two drastically different ideas about how money works. If you were raised in a wealthy environment, then you will most likely raise your children with the principles that lead to and breed wealth. Your children will have different views on life than children living in poverty because of what they see, hear, and feel as they have grown up. Concepts we learn over our lives shape and mold our thinking.

If, however, you were raised in a family where your parents worked a nine-to-five job and punched the time clock each morning, then it's quite possible you have heard more often than not, "You know you're going to have to work for every dime you make." If you were a product of a single parent family in which your mother (or father) worked two or three jobs just to make ends meet, then living paycheck-to-paycheck might be all you know. The environment you were raised in more times than not will dictate how you view life and money.

I have friends who have fought their way out of poverty to create a better life for themselves and their families regardless of how they were raised. It is difficult because they have to change the way they think about life, business, money, and success. Then there are those I coach every day who are striving for success but still struggling. Why? Because what you have seen and heard day in and day out has molded their mindset. Making money and growing a profitable business is not a work problem; it is a thinking problem. Subconsciously, those thoughts drive a deep ravine into the crevices of your soul, and that thinking creates actions, right or wrong, that shapes how you will do business and live your life. The good news is that you have a choice to change how you think.

There is a pattern to growing successful businesses. Whether you know that pattern or not is the question. If you are like me, I didn't know the proper process. Or I will call it "the formula" for doing business right. As a result, the patterns that I set up, or what I thought was right, began to determine my road map. It also created habits in me that were like a steel binding cord that led to anything but what I was wanting to accomplish.

Some people choose to do business in real estate, others in stocks and bonds. For the entrepreneur and small business owner, they want to carve their name in the American Dream. Not only American citizens but thousands around the world come to America in search of fulfilling their lifelong dream of business ownership. Entrepreneurship is the Art of Business. It is learning how to see, feel and trust (SFT) yourself in how to grow a business.

WHAT ARE YOU THINKING?

I am a movie buff, especially films that inspire someone to dream bigger. *Alice Through the Looking Glass* has a great line in it; Johnny Depp's character says, *"Anything is possible if you can believe it is possible."* Believing is a powerful recipe for success. Believing provides hope, and hope is the fuel to fulfilling your destiny. When you lose hope, you lose. Protect your hope; it's as important as your dreams. Keep hope strong by staying around those who celebrate you and your dreams.

Dreams are there to take you further than you have ever been, to go where you've never gone before and do what you've never done. Whether that something is for your children's children or for those around you who are in great need, dreams are there to help you press into something that's about more than yourself. A business that is built to provide new opportunities and services to others. To help someone less fortunate, revive a community or make the world a better place. Isn't that what real living, intentional living is all about?

As important as dreams and hope are to our success, those are still just two ingredients to building a successful organization. I liken it to a chocolate cake recipe. It has several ingredients, like any other recipe, to make it the best it can be. That means the ingredients will need to be properly added at just the right time, with just the right amount of touch, mixed together in the proper order, cooked at the right temperature and handled carefully after it is done in the oven. So does building an organization.

Let's take books, for example. I know a lot about the publishing industry. I have worked with hundreds of authors over my publishing career, and there are things you must do to create a great book. Like a food recipe, it too has a "formula" for success.

> Believe in something larger than yourself…
> Get involved in the big ideas of your time.
> —BARBARA BUSH, former first lady of the U.S.

TIME vs TASKS

We are now living in a time where the traditional model of how we do business has been changed forever. Today, working at home, in your pajamas building a multi-million dollar company is not only possible but currently happening all over the world. Running companies and building organizations while playing in Bora Bora, soaking up the sun on the beach, is easier than ever before. Virtual business is now the norm.

Yet many still think about business, the economy and how to make money the way our parents or even our grandparents knew. The only thing I ever saw, or was told, that my parents did was go to work nine to five, and at the end of the week (or twice a month), they brought home a paycheck. When I began to see there was a different path to success, it was looked down on by those around me. I don't fault them at all because there was not much success they were familiar with seeing outside of the normal lifestyle. They only knew a lot of hard work with little payoff. I had seen more than a few attempts at starting a business, and it didn't end up well.

I was determined to find out the reason behind why some businesses and organizations succeed while others struggle. I have met and coached hundreds of people just like myself who are deeply passionate about the organization we've launched. But then after a few short years, they became disappointed, depressed and lost in the process because it had not turned out like planned. Why is this? I believe it's all in the math. Let me explain.

Donna opened a new tech company three years ago and called our offices to ask if I could help her figure out why she wasn't growing, even though she was doing everything she knew to do. After getting to know Donna, it was clear she was working herself into an early hospital visit, being at the office early, working late, then taking care of all the paperwork after she got home and on weekends. Her goal was to make $350,000 in her business within three years. However, she was barely making $100,000. Her hours were long, she was not getting ahead, her dreams were shattered, and she was afraid of the future.

No matter your educational background, no matter your age, whether you want to make $100,000 this year or $300,000 or even $1 million, it doesn't have anything whatsoever to do with how many hours you work, how long you stay up at night or even what you made last year. There is a simple math equation that would help Donna fix what is broken on her road to successful entrepreneurship. The equation is the same, no matter who you are, or where you live. Those factors are not even relevant.

But here's why we mistakenly think it's relevant: it's because most people equate *money* with *hours* and not tasks. At a certain time in U.S. history, we've come up with two mysterious numbers: eight and forty. We work eight hours a day, five days a week, in order to get a paycheck at the end of a forty-hour work week. We go to work Monday through Friday, work forty hours every week, and pick up a paycheck on the first or fifteenth, because it feels safe.

This is all that Donna has known and seen. She has now taken a risk, stepped out of the normal eight to five to own her own business, but little does she know that the world she has now stepped into operates under ***different rules.***

Why doesn't Donna know this? Because no one ever told her how it works. They didn't teach her in high school or college; she didn't come from an entrepreneurial family. So what did Donna do? She opened her business on the principles and formula that making money and growing a profitable business work on the same system as she has only known: if you work hard from nine to five, at the end of the week or month there will be a paycheck to take home. But in fact, Donna owed more at the end of the week than what was coming in. The math is not the same. In fact, there is a better, much better payoff, as Donna will find out.

For many hard-working individuals, working a standard forty-hour work week is all they have known. And for some it is fairly reliable, as far as it goes. For others and the times we are now living in, it has become less and less reliable. Either way, this standard of working forty hours for someone else, in fact building someone else's dream, is the only way many have known how to make money. Our annual income is eight, times forty, times fifty-two. And we've been trained to accept this fact that it is the only way to make money, when in fact it is NOT. There is a different system and formula to understand as an entrepreneur.

I'm not sure who set up this crazy math equation for all of the masses to follow, but what I am sure about is that making money has nothing whatsoever to do with how many hours you work.

Pay close attention; making this adjustment in your thinking will change the way you do business and the way you can create lifelong residual income for you and your family. When Donna began to understand there was a different formula to making money, and how money works, she began to change her financial future.

If Donna's business is going to grow and succeed, her work week must be based on **tasks.** The small business owner is *task-driven*, rather than hourly driven. I think many aspiring business owners are unaware of how this truly works. I know, because I was.

Creating a successful profitable business, one that is built on a residual income model, has nothing whatsoever to do with the amount of hours worked. Instead, it is based on the principles of *action and reaction*. With the strategic actions that are carefully planned out by Donna, she begins to create a different set of reactions. Where there is the presence of proper actions, there will be a profitable reaction. If the proper actions in your business are taken, then you will see results—increase. It is a measuring stick you can count on.

If you are struggling in your business, then it is simple; you are not doing the **tasks** necessary to create the amount of revenue needed to build successfully. This was Donna's problem. The habits she had created were not moving her any closer to success, only stacking up against her. Trust me, I did it for years and was drowning.

PROPER ACTIONS

When Donna asked me to help her build a strategic master plan that would double her revenue within the next year, it was not only possible, but simple. First, we needed to know what field or industry that she wanted to do business in. Second, determine the total gross revenue she wanted to make. Third, in what amount of time she wanted to make it (which was one year) and fourth, establish the location (local, national, international) she wanted to do business in. Once we have these four hard variables, then we can determine the proper actions, and create a timeline to accomplish those actions. With a mathematical value attached to each action and task, Donna will be able to predict her end-of-year earnings if she stays the course. Hard variables with the right math will set up Donna for a win. A strategic master plan with the correct hard variables and the appropriate actions will provide the desired results. Success is inevitable!

These essential steps—creating a clear, well-defined strategy coupled with the proper math variables—is where turning those big dreams into reality begins. Knowing where you want to go and how you will get there (or not knowing) is how growth (or lack of growth) is created.

Take a moment and judge for yourself in your own business what is happening. The actions that are in motion right now are creating the amount of revenue and growth your business is currently experiencing. It's essential to choose those actions carefully. Plan them out and clearly define what you need to do to create the ripple effect you want to see in twelve, twenty-four and thirty-six months.

BUSINESS HEALTH

Here is a simple exercise to help you evaluate your business's current health. It will require being very honest with yourself.

Where are you financially in your business right now? Stop and really think about this. Are you living the life you are living right now based on your past and present actions? The actions you have taken over the past year are in motion and currently being fulfilled right now as we speak.

Now, if you're working hard and taking a lot of actions, yet you're still not making the kind of money you want to make, then it can only mean one of two things. You're either not taking the proper actions, because you don't know what they are, or you're just not practicing them as you should.

Just as two plus two always equals four—it's a constant—so, too, the proper principles of business are constant. If you take the correct actions, then you will receive the results of successful growth. Learning proper business principles work *if you work them*. Chapter six goes into greater detail on good business principles for success.

CHAPTER SIX

Master Your Business

> I was fearless, I knew I would make it work,
> and that's the difference between successful entrepreneurs
> and those that don't get ahead—it's that tenacity and drive.
> —LORI GREINER, *Shark Tank* Investor and Entrepreneur

Think of your business as a ship that has left port and is in the middle of the ocean headed for the Caribbean Islands. All the elements of the wind, waves and sea affect how that ship moves through the waters. In order to get from one country to another across the Atlantic or Pacific Ocean, there has to be someone on the bridge of that ship to set the course. If there is no navigation set, a ship in the open oceans will never hit its desired destination.

If you get on a ship to take a cruise to the Bahamas and you end up in Haiti, it would not only be very disappointing, but you would have to wonder how much experience the captain of that ship had. You are expecting when you get on a cruise ship that someone knowledgeable and experienced will get you to where the brochure said you would be going. It would be crazy to get on a cruise liner that said they were going somewhere in the Caribbean and end up in Alaska.

In order to have a successful business, you must set a definite course, with clearly defined actions. When my husband and I were in our twenties and thirties, we built a very successful church that is still fulfilling the mission it was intended for. It is one of my greatest accomplishments, and it will continue to bring value to people for many years. It is a part of my legacy, and I'm very proud of the work we did there. While my work currently is in helping for-profit businesses thrive, I continue to have the opportunity to help many nonprofit organizations grow.

Whether you are building a for profit or nonprofit organization, basic business principles work for both, no matter what field or industry you are in. If you want to own your own for-profit business, you can. If you want to work for yourself as a solopreneur, you can. If you want to start your own nonprofit, you can. *How* you set the course is the dividing line between success or failure. Statistically, fifty percent of businesses that open today will be closed in one year, but that is not a business owner's goal when they begin—at least not the ones I talk to. Entrepreneurs want to succeed; they do not want to fail.

So, why are so many not seeing success, especially when it seems like we have the ability to ask anything we need to learn on any platform on the internet? Think about it this way: We are living in an amazing time in history when access to knowledge about anything and everything is literally at our fingertips. Our intake is no longer limited to in-person discourse and lectures.

The information is there for us to access, but the courage to take action on that information is lacking. Maybe it is a fear of failure? Possibly it's merely that you're not sure it will work and you will invest a lot of time and energy with little to no results? Perhaps it's a lack of knowledge in the field of business? You have passion and heart, but maybe you have little to no experience in running a successful organization. That was me—little to no experience in how to create a business that would thrive.

THE KNOWLEDGE YOU NEED IS AVAILABLE

You might not know a thing about starting your own business. Good! Then you will not have as much to unlearn.

What we think we know isn't always what is true—and this can affect how we conduct our business. Whether we were taught about entrepreneurship, studied business in college, or were around people who owned businesses all of our lives, there are a lot of ideas we just naturally picked up during our lives. Some of them are useful, some not so much. What we physically see with our natural eyes is often more powerful than what is communicated to us verbally.

The work of doing business that we see in the individuals who surround us creates a powerful education, whether we realize it or not.

The way we have seen businesses open and then close gives us an education, whether we want it or not. What we see and hear can lead us to make assumptions about business ownership that are not beneficial to us. Many times, failures result from a false understanding of how successful, healthy organizations are started and built. This is why it is so important to have good mentors and coaches around us, so we are able to make our ventures profitable.

A brain surgeon would not even think twice about going into an operating room without first having years of education in the skills he or she needed, hours of practice, internship and much more. They know they need the disciplined mastery of surgical skills in order to be successful in their career, and they take that seriously. Well, starting your own business may not be brain surgery, but receiving a proper education and the understanding of how to start a successful business will put you much farther ahead than if you just began to wing it.

And let me again point out something I just said that I want you to get. It is "the proper education" that will put you far ahead. This does not mean you need to go back to college; You won't get it there. Trust me, I know. You don't get this kind of education sitting in a college classroom studying business. It is not your dreams alone that will make you the kind of money you are looking for. You need the right knowledge, and finding it isn't always easy. Like many business owners I coach each year, when I took over our business, I had a very difficult time knowing who to trust, or where to find the right training and education. I needed to take my business to the next level, and I didn't know anyone who could hold my hand and teach me how.

It was ironic. My husband and I had built a very successful church, yet somehow for me, what we knew how to do in ministry work did not translate into growing a successful for-profit business. I struggled to understand the comparison.

Over the years, I've come to realize I was not alone in that struggle. As I began coaching and meeting small business owners across this country, I realized how little proper education many had to build thriving organizations. Perhaps this explains a statistic that I'm not fond of—three percent of this country creates more wealth than the remaining ninety-seven percent combined. There is something seriously wrong with those numbers. I think we can do better.

The answer isn't necessarily more college. Over one-third of today's billionaires have no formal college education and no degree. Whether you go to college or not does not determine how successful you will or will not become. You may have heard this saying before: "Whether you think you can or you think you can't, you are right." Achieving success is up to you.

Entrepreneurship is not learned in the classroom. Don't get me wrong. As I've said earlier, I believe in education. I have my doctorate, and I teach often at a nearby university. But I also know that even if you sit in a classroom, study hard and get your degree, you will not avoid the journey of discovery and hard knocks that every business owner must take on the road to success. The day-to-day grind that it takes to build, grow and reap the rewards of working as an entrepreneur and small business owner is something you can't avoid.

But you can navigate it more easily, with less errors, when you seek help along the way. You can't do it all on your own; if you could, you would have already done it. The goal is to work smarter and go farther. I believe everyone needs a coach to help get them to the next level in life and in business. When you need help, the coaches at Don't Do Business Alone will help you navigate those day-to-day challenges every business owner faces as they open up for business each day. If you are a leader of a nonprofit or ministry, Don't Do Church Alone is a great resource you can trust for support and growth.

FIND THE RIGHT HELP

Finding the right help, from people who can give you the right advice and positive motivation, will help you gain the ground you're seeking. Sometimes, you'll come across people who don't give you the assistance or advice you need, and you'll need to shake off the experience, and keep seeking what you need. This is one of the reasons I do what I do for other business owners; it's because I know how important it is to get good advice and how disappointing it is when the assistance you seek takes you down the wrong path.

Remember how I was trying to manage my publishing business on my own for the first time in my life? I was struggling and needed to learn. So, I walked into the Small Business Administration (SBA) in my city looking for some direction. Unfortunately, I walked out more discouraged than I had felt when I went in.

I had arranged an appointment with an associate to possibly get some resources for making my business become stable. As I sat across the desk from a woman I expected to help me, she began to tell me how she and her husband owned their own business. I was so glad to talk to someone who was seasoned in entrepreneurship. I thought to myself, "This is going to be great!"

I began to ask her all kinds of questions about their business. What did they do? How did they get started? She answered all of my questions politely. Then I asked her how she liked owning her own business. I wish I had never asked that question.

She said, "Well, to be honest with you, it is really very, very hard. I hate it. We never have enough money or jobs. In fact, I told my husband we just need to close it down. We can barely make it. It's rough!"

Whatever she said after that I did not hear. I just remember thinking, *This is not where I need to be if I'm going to receive business help.* I had gone in excited to find help and hope, only to leave discouraged and disappointed. As I stood up to leave the room, she handed me her information and wished me the best. Needless to say, I dropped all of the information she had given me in the trash as I exited her office. I know there are a ton of great people who work in the SBA organization; this just happened to be the wrong one for me. I am sure she was a really great person and meant well. She simply did not know how to build a successful organization and she needed to get out of that office.

I knew if I was going to survive, I would need to stay as far away from that kind of misinformation as I could. I wanted to be associated with people who were succeeding and had real answers about getting real results. There's a reason it is said that we are who we surround ourselves with. If we hope to gain any amount of success in business, we must get around those who are building thriving organizations. If we want real answers, we need to be around those who have answers that work and create the kind of results we're looking for.

Growing a small business is no small task. I wasn't sure why, but I did feel like I had it in me to build something great. And the truth was, now more than ever I had to figure *'that something'* out. If I didn't, I would be living out of a suitcase or worse, living with my mom. Just kidding, mom! I know she will be reading this and she is truly the best mom in the world. Oh and by the way, she would love it if I lived with her for the rest of my life. However, that is not what I wanted for my future or the future of my kids.

I meet business owners every day who are asking themselves the question, *Do I have what it takes to build a successful organization?* **Yes, you do!** You're just going to need some help getting there. If you could do it on your own, you would have already done it. Don't be embarrassed or shrink back just because you don't know *'the how'* or figured out *'the why'* yet. We don't come out of the womb knowing what it takes to do everything. Some get it earlier than others; some have good role models along the way and see how businesses are run. But for the 97% who start businesses each year, many have not learned all they need to know about the journey of entrepreneurship. We're here to make sure you don't take that journey alone.

When my husband passed unexpectedly, I had never been on my own and I really had no idea how to turn a small business into something that would support us long-term. I don't know that I even knew the word *entrepreneur* or what it really meant. But I did feel like my previous work prepared me for what was ahead. The work I had done for the church with our city. Developing volunteer teams and building a fine arts department where I managed over seventy-five singers and musicians each week. Looking back, my road to entrepreneurship began there, in those days. I was being developed for this season of my life. I just didn't see it when I first began.

Having little to no confidence in my new position as owner and president, I began seeking for answers. Shortly after the funeral and desperately praying, a course of miracle events began to happen. I was contacted by a businessman looking for a speaker to open for him in his new seminar business. I assured him that I did not think I was the person he was looking for, because most of my speaking was inspirational. I had been speaking since I was in my twenties. He paused for a moment and then asked, "Can you speak in front of two hundred people?"

I said, "Yes I can."

He said, " Can you speak in front of twenty thousand people?"

And I said, "Yes I can."

Then he said, "You are exactly what I am looking for. Would you come and sit in one of my seminars to see if it would be a good fit for you?"

I agreed and hung up the phone. A couple of days later, I took the three-hour drive to be a part of one of his events. I joined a group of leaders, professionals and entrepreneurs gathering in a hotel event room to listen to a man I had never met or heard about. He was new to the seminar business, and to my surprise, was one of the best teachers on business I had ever heard. From the time he opened his mouth, this guy was an incredible speaker. I have heard a lot of speakers in my career but he was off-the-charts good.

Needless to say, I began traveling and opening for him in his events. Not only did we educate thousands of small businesses owners from coast to coast, but I got a million dollar education day in and day out. Week after week, month after month. That adds up to a lot of hours sitting in seminars receiving the best elite business education I could ever ask for. My desperate prayers and long, sleepless nights of grief turned into what I dreamed of building: a small business coaching and consulting firm with state-of-the-art software that is not only affordable but helping business owners all over the world.

DECISIVE CHOICES ARE POWERFUL

Decide today that you will not just become good, but great at what you do. I would like you to take a moment to get a pen and paper out, open up your notes app or if you bought one of my paperback books, flip to the back of the page and make a list. I want you to make a list of the top twenty-five goals you want to accomplish within the next three years in three areas:

1. Personally: What do you want to look like or become in the next three years?

2. Relationships: What kinds of relationships do you want to have around you?

3. Business: What do you want your business to look like in three years? What kind of revenue do you want your business to be making? What do you want to be selling and to whom?

Now, begin to work backwards from that mark. Ask yourself, "What would it take to reach those goals? What one step should you take today to move closer to that goal?" Then figure out what is the next step… and then the next. Map it all out on paper. Write it down, and make it so plain that anyone who read it could follow you.

Reverse the process. Instead of starting from front to back ("here's where I am now and here's where I want to go"), flip your plan upside down and work from back to front ("here's where I want to go; how do I get there?"). Working out a path with the end point in mind will give the proper steps you need to take to meet those goals and accomplish your dreams. This works on any business or life plan. When you begin to master your business and not let your business days master you, then you will begin to see real results!

Decide right now that you are going to begin to take the proper steps toward fulfilling your goals. Keep one focus in mind: to accomplish that three-year plan. You're not going to know everything you need to know in the beginning. You're going to start, then refine, tweak and move along the way. It's going to be hard in the beginning because small businesses are not an easy task. In fact, it is unrealistic to think you're going to do everything right in the beginning. But we'll be here to help you not go it alone.

It is no accident that you're here reading this book or have downloaded the ebook. You are here just like I was when that voice on the other end of the phone called me that day, at just the right time, to ask me just the right questions that set a plan in motion. That was the door of opportunity that day, and I stepped through it to begin a new journey of success and security.

There is real power in solid decision making. Determine that you will do whatever it takes to outlast the challenges, and as my business partner says, "*But* doesn't exist." Whatever you want, write it down, set your mark, and go get it.

CHAPTER SEVEN

Write the Vision

> To step toward your destiny, you have to
> step away from your security.
> —CRAIG GRESHEL, author and pastor

Entrepreneurs are some of the hardest working people you will ever meet. But just like me, the lack of education for most business owners on how to grow a business is missing. After all, whoever taught us how to run a successful organization? I definitely did not learn it in high school. In fact, I don't remember even hearing the word *entrepreneur*.

A couple of times each year, I visit a dear friend of mine in Las Vegas. All you have to do is look around at the casinos, shops and restaurants to see that there is plenty of money passing from hand to hand. It's clear money hasn't gone anywhere, and you have every right to make as much of it as you want to—or as little as you want to. It is the American Dream for many! Once you have made the amount you desire, you can decide to do with it what you want to. You can keep it, or spend it. You may want to donate it to a favorite charity or church, or use it to solve global medical issues and provide education worldwide.

The challenge today isn't the lack of money itself, but rather the constant untruths that permeate our society and our thinking, particularly when it comes to creating wealth and making more money. We are constantly bombarded by people telling us, "Money isn't everything." "Don't ever expect to get paid for what you're worth." "You're living in a dream world if you think that you can have everything you want."

Make no mistake, money isn't everything, but money will solve a lot of problems. Many have been taught to be satisfied with making *just enough*. Our ability to build a successful organization, make more money and create long-term wealth isn't evil. *It's smart!*

Too many people today are living paycheck to paycheck. It is no secret that many families are struggling to put food on the table for their kids. However, anyone who has a desire to get out of the rat race of "barely getting along" can do so. With the right education and the proper tools, you can start and grow your own successful organization, take control of your future and create greater opportunities for you and your family. With the right books, podcasts and internet education, a person has every opportunity to receive the kind of education it takes to become successful in their chosen field and industry.

Regardless of what you may think or what people may be saying today, *this* economy is your friend. You have the greatest opportunity than ever before, right now, today to begin to build your dream.

YOU NEED A MAP

Creating a proper strategy is by far one of the most important factors in developing a business that will succeed. I will go on to say that creating a mindful plan for *your life* alongside a strategic business master-plan is one of the smartest decisions you could ever make. I encourage you to do this! So, let's get started.

Keep in mind that without a clear roadmap, the challenges will begin to stack up with no end in sight.

I have friends right now who are struggling with their business and can't understand why. Having *no real* working master plan for growing a business is like getting in your car for a cross country road trip without having a roadmap, or turning on your GPS. What I mean by "working plan" is very simple—I mean, one that is mapped out, thought through, and written down. Don't get me wrong; I don't mean that you have to have it all figured out before starting. In fact, most people will never start if they wait on everything to line up. Most of my team knows I will jump in feet first as fast as I can when I see opportunity. But for the most part, I have thought it through thoroughly, mapped it out in my head and written down the framework.

In 2015, I set out on a roadtrip to drive from Tulsa, Oklahoma to Vancouver, Washington to visit my brother and sister-in-law. You may not know this, but it is 2,059 miles from Tulsa to Vancouver. A long way! It was the best trip I ever took, and I enjoyed every minute with my girlfriend "Thelma" (real name Carol). We felt like Thelma and Louise on a road trip; we just never planned on driving off the cliff. Before setting out, we traced the shortest distance from our current location to my brother's address. We planned out how long we wanted to drive each day, what cities we wanted to stay all night in, reserved our hotel rooms in those cities, and scheduled what time approximately we would arrive. We scheduled the particular sites we wanted to see along the way and what time we would get into Vancouver.

Starting a business is like getting in a car headed for a distant city. For driving, you need to map out the road you're going to take, what car you want to take, and how long you're going to need to drive each day. For business, you'll draw up a marketing and sales plan, which you'll need to sell your product, in order to make the kind of money you want to make. You'll need to be clear about what field or industry you will be working in, what tools you will need, how many sales it's going to require.

It has been my experience that most people go into business without even thinking about what road they are going to take, let alone plan out the particulars. We begin with a passion and think if we build it, they (the customers) will come. We don't do the proper research, add up the numbers, or know what will get us to profitability, or what it's going to take to get where we want to be. Then when we encounter problems, or crash and burn, we wonder why. Statistically, ninety percent of businesses that open have no real written master plan that will build long-term success. That is ludicrous!

So let me ask you: Do you have a real plan for your business? Or are you just hoping that the actions you take today are going to turn into something better tomorrow? You can't keep doing the same thing over and over again and expect different results. Evaluate what you're doing now and make the adjustments necessary so you can arrive where you want your business to end up. Let's get off that road to nowhere and build a new highway to success.

A WORKING PLAN

Whether you realize it or not, we are all working off of a business plan of some kind. Whether it is working or not, whether it is in our head or on paper, we're all working off a plan. You may not even realize it is a plan, but you have set up a system that is in motion, unintentionally or intentionally. If you are seeing an increase in your client base and revenue, then the plan you are using is working. If not, then it has too many holes in it—and no matter how hard you work at it, until you fix those holes there will be problems. I liken it to a puzzle. If you fit all of the pieces of a puzzle together but are missing a few in the middle, it will never be complete until you find those missing pieces.

Let's assume you don't have a well-written master plan in the first place, which is the case with most businesses I coach each year.

Most of us have been told the way to write a business plan is to begin with your vision, followed by a mission statement, then the marketing strategy, and it goes on from there. Everything changed for me and my thinking when I heard someone say, "That approach will *never* work. In fact, it's mathematically impossible to grow a thriving organization with that approach."

Just think about it for a moment. You write all of this information down—your vision, your mission, your marketing strategy, S.W.O.T analysis (strengths, weaknesses, opportunities and threats), how much staff you want to hire, the building you want to buy, and on and on the list goes. Then, at the very bottom, you roll the dice for it to hopefully add up to a number you want to magically create. For most people, it is that magic number of one million dollars.

If you are a math student, or even if you know basic math, you would see how that couldn't possibly work. Two plus two equals four, all the time. It can't, and doesn't, ever equal five. So how can it work for a random group of words like a vision, a mission, and a guess on how you are going to market your business to equal an exact number you have chosen at the bottom of your business plan? A business plan is a set of numbers that equal a *solution*. In fact, ninety percent of business owners and entrepreneurs I meet every year have never even equated a business plan to a group of numbers that add up to profit and loss, yet that is what an organization is composed of: a group of numbers, plus actions, causing a set of reactions, that equal income.

The first thing to do is, flip your business plan upside down and begin to build it from *back* to *front*. This will give you the proper ceiling to work with. Every business has a ceiling, and there is no way to out-earn it.

Remember, the same rules for earning and growth apply to all of us. Because of the way mathematics work, when you gather hard variables and set them in motion, you create an inevitable outcome. That inevitable outcome is based on the variables you select and how you choose to add, subtract, multiply, and divide them. Until you know what the ceiling is, you will constantly be operating based on assumptions (and most of the time, they will be false assumptions). So, how could you really know if you are taking the proper actions, unless you work backwards from your ceiling of earning potential?

Let's say you're a runner in training. You live on Main Street, and your coach calls and says, "Hey! I'm on Main Street. Run until you see me, and hurry up!" When you leave, if you don't know your coach's exact location, it would be impossible to know which direction to run, what supplies you may need, what pace to set for yourself, how hard to take the hills, and how long it would take you to find him. In other words, it would be impossible to take the correct actions because you don't know how far down Main Street your coach really is. In other words, there aren't enough fixed variables to help you make good decisions.

On the other hand, if your coach calls and says, "You live on Main Street, right? Head North on Main and run until you see me. I'm exactly three miles from your house. Hurry up; I'm out of gas." Now you know exactly where you're going, the proper direction, how hard you must push, and what supplies you need to bring with you. An absolutely necessary key to business success is picking your ceiling. You have to know your hard variables first, and they will give you the *proper* "how."

Consider this: When my husband and I began our first business, one aspect of the plan was to begin publishing our own books, along with books of other authors who wanted to get published. For many years, we were working on this aspect of the plan from front to back. Each publication we produced was designed to get us closer to our final objective and goals. Since we were behind in 2007, we were forced to figure out what was wrong with the way we were doing business and why we weren't able to hit our expected goals, which were double the revenue we were currently bringing in.

Then in 2009, after my husband passed away, I really had to get serious. How would I meet my personal and business revenue goals without working sixteen hours a day? I knew if I kept doing what I was doing, the way we had always been doing things, I would be in the hospital by the end of the year—exhausted. The truth is, we had tried many times before to work harder and longer, thinking the answer was just that—if we would work more hours, and determine to work a little harder, that would somehow create more revenue. That was just stupid!

Working more hours will *never* solve your problem.

This situation forced me to lock down the second and most important variable: what would it take to create more revenue than I was currently making without working more hours? I was now a working single mom with a teenager. Working more hours was not the answer, and somehow I knew that wouldn't work. I had to find better answers.

CHAPTER EIGHT

Your Next Level

> Good leaders are not born, they are
> people who try hard to be exceptional.
> —BARBARA CORCORAN, Real Estate Mogul and
> *Shark Tank* Investor

Too many business owners today are working too hard for too long and not seeing the kind of results they should be producing. There is a better plan of action than working all hours of the night until you drop. You must know your numbers. There are four questions you need to address:

1. How much money do you want to make?
2. In what amount of time do you want to make it?
3. In what industry?
4. What geographical location (city, state, national, international)?

Once you answer these four questions, you now have some hard variables to work with. Let's begin with the end in mind. You now know how much money you want to make, the fixed time frame to achieve it, what industry you want to be a part of and where you want to do business. Now you have a set of measurable factors to work with. Once you know how much money you want to make, in what amount of time, and in what field, then you can begin to build a master plan that will produce a desired set of outcomes. This gives you the *proper* amount of product you need, the *proper* number of employees to hire, the *proper* number of contracts you need to secure, the *proper* size of the building you need, the *proper* price points to buy and sell at, and the *proper* marketing strategy that will capture that exact figure. Anything else is simply a *guess*. Anything less, and you are just winging it.

Can you see how your success is not based on how hard you work, how many hours you put in, how many more people you hire, or even the state of the economy? The fact is, with these hard variables, you can choose the amount of hours you want to work and how to make that happen. It is all based on correct math: addition, subtraction, multiplication and division.

When I became president of our book publishing company, what I needed more than an investor was the answer to these simple but very important questions. My answer wasn't more hours or more investment; what I needed was to build a master plan with a very specific set of numbers. Then I would have something to work with. With those questions answered, building a business plan, from *back* to *front,* would produce the desired goals and create success.

This approach creates a road map that shows the *appropriate* tools needed and the *proper* math that would provide the revenue necessary to grow and sustain the organization. With those hard variables, I now knew how many authors we would need to secure, what size of staff we needed to complete the jobs, what kind of production line, and the amount of equipment.

The outcome? Within the first three months, I began to triple my profits, and by the end of the year I had paid off all the equipment in our 4,200 square foot publishing facility. This was a huge accomplishment, and best of all—*it works*!

PUTTING INTO PRACTICE

If someone asked me to do a business plan for a new startup nail salon, I would begin by asking the owner these four simple questions. Keep in mind, the same four questions apply to any business. The industry doesn't matter and the equation doesn't change. These questions will give you the first and most important hard variables you need for long-term success.

Let's say the new business owner's name is Lynn, and she wants to make one million dollars in three years in her new venture. We see she has questions number one, two, and three already answered. But she doesn't know if this particular industry could yield that much money in that amount of time.

So, the next step is to do some research into the industry to answer question number four. What Lynn needs to know is, can a nail salon capture one million dollars in revenue in a three-year period? Is that even possible? Can she do that many manicures and pedicures in that amount of time to capture that volume of revenue? Is it even possible?

Through research, we can learn what the average nail salon business is making per year and approximately how many manicures and pedicures they can do in a month, or a year. The result is that these businesses are typically yielding much less than one million dollars in revenue within that amount of time. I know a little bit about the nail salon businesses because I owned one when I was in my twenties.

Are there some people in the nail salon industry capturing that volume or more per year? Yes. Is it possible for Lynn? Absolutely. However, she cannot only do manicures and pedicures in the current location she has picked out. And working more hours will not get her there, nor will working longer hours each day.

So, what is the answer without forcing Lynn to ditch her dream? For Lynn, we would create a plan that includes opening multiple stores, franchising, or providing a training school component to her current model. This will not only allow her to work in the field that she is passionate about, but will also give her the opportunity to achieve her goals and fulfill her dream.

If Lynn had not answered all four of these questions in the beginning, she would have never known this. Within a few years, she would have been frustrated and probably closing her doors, discouraged. There would have been no way Lynn could accomplish her goals following her current game plan. But because she has done her homework, she will be able to build a business model that positions her business for success.

Keep in mind that unless you are completely committed and passionate about what you are building, your long-term success will be limited. I heard Steve Jobs say, "Business is really, really hard stuff. If you don't love what you do, the smartest thing you can do is get out. And you would be absolutely right to do so." Loving what you do is the fuel that will give you the endurance you need to go the distance and overcome the challenges you will face along the way. Make sure all four questions are answered before you move forward.

DO YOUR RESEARCH

Ultimately, if you are trying to hit a monetary mark in a certain time frame, you should do some very specific research. Separating yourself from the pack and positioning yourself into the top ten percent of your industry, even in a new field, is much better than placing yourself in a saturated market. It is important to study your industry and choose a field where hitting your desired mark is not only possible but probably. You want to be in the top ten to twelve percent of your industry.

Currently, I do quite a bit of writing and publishing for new authors, experienced speakers, and educated entrepreneurs. Many have a desire to become a best-selling author. Some have hit the bestseller list. Others have worked on selling their stories to film companies, producers or as a screenplay, with hopes that their story will someday land in theaters.

Becoming a best-selling author in the publishing industry is more than difficult because of the amount of books being written and authors seeking bestseller status. If you choose to pursue this field, and many do, it is very important to create opportunities that will set yourself apart. For instance, hire a professional editor to edit your book instead of going it alone. An editor who already has a track record for working on best-selling books will increase your odds. Many new authors say to me that they don't need an editor because they are using their sister or aunt who is a high school English teacher. While that person may be very good and qualified to teach English, that is a very different field than a professional editor who has several best-selling books on their resume.

You will also need to seek out an experienced designer to design your book cover to attract the kind of attention necessary for mass publication. A book is judged by its cover—no doubt about it. Next, a marketing firm that has experience in advertising, marketing, and promotion of newly released books will provide greater opportunity. Do you see how important research becomes before ever putting pen to paper?

These are just a few examples of entrepreneurs seeking to build businesses in their own area of passion.

Whichever field you are seeking to grow your business in, find the best in that field and do what they are doing. As you study and learn, be careful not to simply chase the next new fad, the next new motivational seminar, the next new coach in town. Instead, find a coach or mentor, whether it's someone who will hold your hand and teach you business or someone you follow religiously online. Look for someone who has started, owned and grown their own business, and has the level of success you want to have. Specifically. follow someone who is accomplishing the success you are looking to accomplish but is farther ahead than you are.

For example, if you are making money as a business owner, don't look for a mentor who is making money trading stocks. Most likely, they will know very little about the details of how a business gets customers to walk through the doors. Attend seminars where they are speaking, watch what they are posting on social media, and surround yourself with those who are the most successful in their field.

Once you have been intentional in these areas, set some hard variables to define where you want to be in what amount of time. Decide how much money you want to earn within one year, in the next three years, and in the next five years. Be sure that you have chosen a field you are passionate about and very confident in. Then go for it. You have now begun to set the correct math in motion.

FOREVER MOVING FORWARD

The world of business is changing rapidly. Once you have your first few key variables, get moving! You can figure out the rest of the details along the way. Most people wait to have the majority of the "how" answered before they begin. You don't need to have all of the "how" collected, just these key principles. If you have read the previous chapters, you are well on your way to being ahead of the game.

CHAPTER NINE

Direct Sales

I have never worked a day in my life without selling.
There is no such thing as an entrepreneur with no selling skills.
—ESTÉE LAUDER, founder of Estee Lauder
Companies & Cosmetics

Direct selling is a term that is used for person-to-person selling in locations other than a retail establishment. It refers to sales that are generated through one individual salesperson, whether working from home or for a business, or a team of trained salespersons, all who call directly on prospective customers. There is a direct, personal gathering of leads, preparing presentations, developing demonstrations, and the sale of products and services to consumers, one-on-one to individuals or to organizations.

I can't emphasize this strongly enough, nor can I repeat it too many times. Sales and the profession of sales provide anyone the opportunity to create their own success in any economy. Sales is the lifeblood of any and all businesses. Once you develop the skills necessary to be good at it, you will never look back or lack in creating revenue. A team of passionate *Relational Client Representatives* (our team of sales professionals) is the backbone to our business growth.

I have never forgotten what I learned as I began my entrepreneurial journey:

> Sales is a profession, not a job.
> —EDWARD HARDING, author of *The Lost Art of Direct Sales*

I took that lesson to heart and made it part of my focus as I built my businesses. It was difficult at first because all I could think about while sitting in business seminars was that I didn't want to be *that salesperson*. You know—that one who no one wants to see coming.

Let me help dial it down for you. You're only that person if you want to be. But if you want to create real relationships with real people, develop lasting customers who want to grow their services and provide good products for their clients, give others new opportunities, provide masterful education, introduce families to new products that help them live longer and better, then you will never be *that person*.

It has become the best part of my life to meet new people and create lasting relationships that are important to me for the rest of my life.

It is the reason I coach people, consult organizations and help people fulfill their destiny.

For most of us, we began our business with a dream, a passion and a desire. I said this earlier, but it bears repeating again: there is a misconception that if you build it (a business), they (customers) will come, much like the 1989 movie, *Field of Dreams*. I know; I had this illusion myself. This belief is just that—a misconception. So don't be shy in promoting what you can do, build or have developed. And when they don't come, and all of your hard work seems to be for nothing, and discouragement sets in, then keep developing your skills of selling, learn to promote better, and build a better presentation than you did last year, last month, or last week.

In order to take my business to the next level after the death of my husband, it was going to require a different set of actions, and I knew that. I was aware we had grown it as far as it was going to go with the education and knowledge I currently had. And now it was time to expand. I had to grow; my livelihood depended on it. The actions we had taken in the past had not gotten us where we wanted to be and I knew it. Change is hard when you're unsure what the future holds, but the risk was worth it, and I stepped into the unknown.

ACTION vs REACTION

So how do you create a continuous flow of customers who love your company, love your product, and return to purchase time and again? We all know that what goes up must come down. It is the law of gravity. The actions we take today create desired or undesirable reactions tomorrow. If I hit the call button on my cell phone, there will be a reaction—a call will be made to someone. If I jump out of a plane without a parachute, I will fall fast to the ground. If I dive into a pool, the water will splash—it has to splash. There will be a reaction to the action. It is a law of physics. The actions you and I take today—right or wrong—create reactions.

Newton's third law of action vs. reaction states there is an equal and opposite reaction to every action. In every interaction, there is a pair of forces acting on the two interacting objects. The size of the forces on the first object equals the size of the force on the second object. Stay with me on this, because it will connect the laws.

If one is available, go ahead and grab a large bowl out of your cabinet and fill it with water. Now take your finger and tap the water's surface. You will see a small ripple circulate to the edge of the bowl. The harder you tap the water, the larger the corresponding ripple out to the edge of the bowl. Now, take your whole hand and slap the water as hard as you can. You might want to do this outside or in a sink, because it's going to get messy. What happens? Your hand slapping the water creates a reaction in the water. The force exerted by your hand upon the water equals the magnitude of the reaction that the water takes in the opposite direction.

Creating a continuous flow of customers is the reaction of a set of properly and strategically developed actions equal to the magnitude of the reaction you are looking for. Here is what I have found out. When you start your business, you work really hard to get things ready to open for business and in a sense, get the lights turned on. Those actions set into motion a set of reactions to come. Those may have been very new actions you had never taken before.

Or, maybe you are a seasoned entrepreneur, but you are stuck and have created a ceiling you don't know how to break through. To go to the next level, it will require a new set of actions—bigger actions. More time commitment, more staff, more accountability, new habits put in place in your own life, new processes, more education; this may require all or some to go where you want to do. There is a new set of actions necessary to create new reactions to lead you into your next step of increase.

Among one of the earliest clients we had after opening our new coaching and consulting firm, Don't Do Business Alone, was a female franchise owner we'll call Sally. Her entrepreneurial venture was running a new franchise she had recently purchased. Her goal was to triple business sales within the next twelve months. We worked the math backwards to find the number of potential prospects she would need to touch or contact in order to reap the amount of revenue she wanted to make.

There is a formula to sales. Revenue is generated by multiplying the number of products sold by the sales produced:

$$\text{Sales Revenue} = \text{Units Sold} \times \text{Sales Price}$$

The more sales a business makes, the more money flows through the business. Whether you sell a service or a product, it is the same. In order to increase sales, you must obtain or produce leads. This is called lead generation. Lead generation is the action or process of identifying, qualifying and cultivating potential customers for a business's products or services.

How many leads do you need to win a sale? There is a basic formula you can count on to help you measure this:

Divide the number of new customers by the lead to customer conversion rate (2%). Based on this formula, you will need 2,500 new leads to create 50 new customers. Whether you have a product or service, the formula works the same *(based on sales averages).*

These are simple math equations that will help you know how many people you need to reach out to and touch each week, each month, each week to create the results you are looking for. First of all, begin with the end in mind. And let me say this first before we really get into it. You're going to have to ditch the thinking that you're not good at math or you hate math. If you hate math, then you ultimately hate money because money is math. It is all in your mindset—change it! Don't be afraid of numbers or what is in your bank account. If that is the case, it is time to face it head on so you can fix it.

Acknowledging where you are at and that you need to change your thinking is the first step to your success. If you are afraid of it—face it! If you procrastinate—acknowledge it! Once you face your fears head on, then you can fix it.

Business is all about math equations, just like music is a math equation. I know because I have played the piano for most of my adult life. It is a group of numbers, plus units of products developed or services provided, combined with a total number of individuals (team members), that equal revenue and profits. This is a math equation that you should not be afraid of and must get very familiar with.

LOVING IT!

I encourage you to embrace the idea of selling as a relational action. Even if it is currently uncomfortable for you, you can learn to love it. I remember the first real business seminar I attended. I had just become an apprentice and began sitting in on classes to learn my way up in the world of successful entrepreneurship. As the instructor spoke about sales, he asked for questions from those who were in attendance. I raised my hand and said that I wanted to build a business, but I really didn't want to do **"the whole sales thing."** He smiled and replied, "That's fine, but then you will have no money!"

I know that seems harsh, but it really put it in perspective for me. Either get a job and build someone else's dream while working your business as a hobby (because that is what you are really doing), or take the leap to build your own dream and secure your own financial future.

If you have a product and you want someone to buy it, you will need to learn how to sell it. The only other way than learning how to sell your product is teaching someone else how to sell it, which requires your participation and involvement anyway. Ultimately, whether you are the product (such as a keynote speaker or author) or whether you have a product (like bath oil and soap) or a service (such as coaching), I believe direct sales is the pathway to growth and success for any organization.

RELATIONAL SALES

As a small business owner, 80 percent of your time should be spent on sales, customer service and focused marketing. The other percentage can then be devoted to administrative duties. When you begin to think this way, you will begin to create lasting results and real success. Many business owners we coach each year either do not understand how to properly sell their product, or they are just not willing to do what it takes to personally promote their product or service. I encourage you to look at sales as building relationships and serving people; then I believe it will take the stigma out of what we have subconsciously believed sales to be.

We tend to think of sales as a calling or gift that only a few have the skills to achieve. But the truth is, we all sell something every day. Even in normal conversations, we sell our ideas and way of thinking. Moms are masters at selling to their kids in order to get them to eat their vegetables, or do chores. Of course, they do it in their children's best interest. But it's still sales.

At Don't Do Business Alone, we teach a sales program titled *7 Steps to Successful Selling*. There is an effective selling process and formula that will help you close more deals and make more money, while building great relationships with customers, clients and organizations. *Please feel free to check it out on our website at www.dontdobusinessalone.com.*

So let's do a quick review of this chapter. The sales actions you take today will have a direct impact on your life and business in the future—action vs reaction. What you see in your business bank account today, tomorrow, the day after tomorrow, and the day after that is a direct result of your actions. If you want more of your product or service sold, then you will want to become a master at selling it. It's very simple. I'm not saying it is easy, just simple. If you make it all about people, building relationships, helping to solve problems and offering great customer service, you will begin to build a different mindset. When you do this, you move from *hoping* to grow to *creating* growth.

CHAPTER TEN

Enjoy The Journey

Get clear on what truly motivates you.
Be true to who you really are,
and realize you are okay just as you.
Dream big and stay committed to what you love to do
as you realize your true potential
to positively impact the world.
—KATRINA RADKE, Olympic Swimmer;
CEO and President of Olympian Performance, Inc.

In my early twenties, I had the opportunity to travel the U.S. with some of the most outstanding speakers and teachers. I did not realize at the time how the experience was shaping me, but it did. There was so much I took for granted, yet the whole time I was traveling with these successful teachers, success was building up in my life, brick by brick. I was connected with people who created an imprint in my life. And then my husband and I settled down to raise our family with a very special group of people who taught us more than we ever taught them. Their lives were changed and ours were too, because we took the opportunity that presented itself to us.

Little did I know that what I did all those years ago would shape me into what I am doing today. But isn't it always that way? I'm sure you've experienced similar moments in your life, where you crossed paths with someone who influenced you?

It's happening right now. Your journey has brought you to this place, at this time, to read this book, and to help you do what you are destined to do. Don't miss your moment. I speak from experience. Many times, because we have our own agenda, our own plans, we miss some of our most important life-changing opportunities. Be intentional about your business and life dreams, and draw a circle around them. Protect them, and act on them. It just might change your life if you really become intentional about where you are right now, doing what you are doing at this moment with the people who are in your life.

> Everybody's not going to understand where you are going, but that is not an excuse for you to not go there.
> —CECE WINANS, Grammy award-winning Gospel singer

TREASURE YOUR RELATIONSHIPS

Over the years, I have established churches, built several businesses and coached hundreds of entrepreneurs. Along the way, I've learned that the greatest opportunity we have in life is not actually *just* to do business—sometimes it's to build great relationships and enjoy the journey of life together. If we can take the stress out of where we are trying to go, then we can enjoy the trip along the way. Trust me, I was really bad at this, but I have learned to be present.

Building a business is hard work and demands a lot of sacrifice. You'll encounter some bumps and bruises along the way. But it is your destiny, so own it. It is your journey and what you are called to do. When you settle that, then begin to master it. Build your skills and master your plan. Once you do that, you'll begin to enjoy the journey that you're on.

If we only realized how important our dreams are to building a brighter future for those around us and the ones we are supposed to touch in this life, we would not hold back for one moment. You don't have to wait to start giving, reaching out, and helping others in need. If you will find a way to help more people with the gifts and talents you have, with the product or service you provide, you can and will find a way to personal wealth.

What is possible is far greater than what is not possible. Don't talk yourself out of your dreams, and certainly don't let anyone else do it. Your dreams are built inside of you to give you a greater quality of life that you can both enjoy and then share with others.

I want to remind you as you are on your road to success that wealth is not found in just money alone. As business owners and entrepreneurs, we can get caught up in the work, losing focus on what matters most. The memories I made with my husband for twenty-eight years are invaluable. Nothing can come close to replacing the fulfillment I have in the life we lived together. Those times are loads and loads of wealth to me. Wealth that money can't buy.

When you come face to face with death like I have, the memories you make in this life mean even more to you. What matters most are the lifelong relationships we built, the joy of watching our boys grow up, their voices laughing, taking them to Disney World, and riding the rides with them. What matters is both the work we built together and the people we poured our lives into. With all of the love, faith, opportunities, health, and friends around us, instead of waiting to become rich, I think we should start from rich and build from there.

In order to live big, you have to live intentionally. You can live by default or by design. You might not always know how to get on the other side of success, but if you will work at it and seek out the proper education, then success will find you.

> I work like it depends on me and
> pray like it depends on God.
> —MARK BATTERSON, *New York Times* bestselling author and pastor

We all know that there are doors we could never have opened or made happen on our own if it had not been for divine intervention. We were in the right place at the right time. Some call it luck. Others call it the universe. I call it the Divine Creator. While doing all we knew to do, someone behind the scenes, outside of our own scheduled planning, made sure we were in the right place at the right time to thrust us into our next chapter of life and business.

At that moment, you are given the best three minutes behind the glass every musician is looking for. To play the music you have always wanted to play for that one you always wanted to play for. That melody you have been working your whole life on. It is now up to you how you're going to play it. The world is your playing field, not just your neighborhood, city or state. Get busy dreaming big and living intentionally about where you want to be. You can write your own music, you can play your own song, you can live the life you always wanted to live, and live it big or live it small. If you can dream it, then go do something about it. It may be that you need to take a class, get a business plan ready, find a coach that will help you go to the next level, or it may be that you just need to make a decision to begin. Whatever it is, now is the time to take that next step and become the best version of yourself.

I hope you will follow my advice and not sit on your dreams! It is not always easy. I particularly like driving the highway when I set out on a trip. It's smooth, in a straight line and mapped out for me. Life is not always that way and hasn't been easy for me. There are a lot of dirt roads that entrepreneurs plow. That can make it really hard. I encourage you to be intentional along the way, to stop and be present, even if it is for just a second, to not let that moment pass without you taking notice. Life can be complicated and not always in a straight line, which I wish it would be. However, *I would rather be somewhere that I want to be, than not to be somewhere I could have been.* I look forward to hearing from you and how your business journey on the road to success is unfolding.

There are men and women who have broken records, built new technology, written life-changing songs, danced their way to stardom, produced legendary films, built great companies, and inspired us all to put our dreams to the test. It is time for you to chase your entrepreneurial dream. You will probably need some help like I did, so I invite you to reach out to me and my team. I believe it is much more fun to do business together than alone. I will tell you this: I learned more working with a personal business coach than I ever did all the years of doing business on my own. We all need someone to get in the ring with us and help us go where we have never gone before. To push us beyond our own self limitations. There is much, much more you can do than you think. You have greater potential than you know. You deserve to capture the business dreams you are chasing. I have done it; *you can too*.

We're friends now, and I would love nothing more than to help you build your dream business. Let's Dream Big and Live Big together!

TO YOUR SUCCESS

Visit the Dr. Margo Bush author page at
www.bushpublishing.com

For business coaching and consulting,
Dr. Margo Bush can be reached at
405-492-2805 or at
drmargo@dontdobusinessalone.com